150
BAKING
recipes

INSPIRED IDEAS FOR
EVERYDAY COOKING

150
CAKE
recipes

INSPIRED IDEAS FOR
EVERYDAY COOKING

recipes

& MUFFIN
recipes

150
FAST
& SIMPLE
recipes

150
GRANDMA'S
recipes

INSPIRED IDEAS FOR
EVERYDAY COOKING

150
HEALTHY
recipes

INSPIRED IDEAS FOR
EVERYDAY COOKING

150
INDIAN
recipes

INSPIRED IDEAS FOR
EVERYDAY COOKING

150
ONE-POT
recipes

INSPIRED IDEAS FOR
EVERYDAY COOKING

150
PASTA
recipes

INSPIRED IDEAS FOR
EVERYDAY COOKING

150
SLOW
COOKER
recipes

INSPIRED IDEAS FOR
EVERYDAY COOKING

150
STIR-FRY
recipes

INSPIRED IDEAS FOR
EVERYDAY COOKING

150
STUDENT
recipes

INSPIRED IDEAS FOR
EVERYDAY COOKING

150
TAPAS
recipes

INSPIRED IDEAS FOR
EVERYDAY COOKING

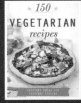

150
VEGETARIAN
recipes

INSPIRED IDEAS FOR
EVERYDAY COOKING

150

HEALTHY
recipes

INSPIRED IDEAS FOR
EVERYDAY COOKING

CONTENTS

INTRODUCTION

A healthy, balanced diet will provide your body with the correct amount of energy and, combined with regular exercise, will make you feel fit, energised and in control of your weight. If this wasn't enough, a healthy eating plan also improves your overall wellbeing and helps to reduce the risk of developing illnesses such as heart disease, obesity, some cancers, strokes and diabetes.

A wholesome diet is also a varied one and should include a variety of food from the main food groups in varying quantities, including fruit and vegetables, starchy complex carbohydrates, proteins and some unsaturated fats. It is also important to include fibre (especially soluble fibre). You should aim to eat at least five portions of a variety of fruit and vegetables every day, but foods high in fat (especially saturated fats), sugar or salt should be limited. Drinking plenty of fluids (such as water and other drinks) each day is vital for good health too.

Remember that eating healthily need never be boring or dull, and this

comprehensive collection of recipes illustrates just how delicious and nutritious healthy recipes can be without compromising on flavour. We include an inspirational selection of wholesome recipes bursting with flavour and appeal, so you can create tasty, nourishing dishes for every day without any fuss. Preparing foods yourself from scratch also means you'll know exactly what you're eating.

To get your day off to a good start we begin with an appetizing assortment of sweet and savoury healthy breakfasts. We include fabulous frittatas and fruity favourites, as well as wholesome porridges packed with goodness. If a pick-me-up power drink is more your morning style, Muesli Motivator Juice or Super Smoothie are great choices.

Next up is a super selection of sustaining snacks and sides, including pâtés, popcorn, crisps, bites and dips. Top picks include nourishing nuggets like Fig & Oat Bites and Roasted Kale Crisps, or nutritious vegetable sides such as Roasted Root Vegetables and Spiced Carrot Mash.

Tuck into a nourishing lunch and choose from our enticing collection of nutrient-rich dishes, which includes wholesome soups, vibrant salads and slaws, healthy burgers and bruschetta, plus ever-popular pizzas and paninis. Enjoy classic weeknight pleasers like Moroccan Meatballs and Chicken Satay Skewers, or try something new like Turkey Farro Salad or Crayfish Cakes.

Our next chapter featuring flavour-packed dinners includes a tempting choice of hearty vegetable, fish and meat-packed mains. Tantalise your taste buds with family favourites like Jerk Chicken or Spaghetti Bolognese, or opt for fabulous fishy dishes like Seafood Stew or Scallops with Lime & Chilli Sauce.

Finally we focus on a scrumptious selection of healthier desserts and bakes, perfect for satisfying a sweet tooth. We feature an amazing choice of delectable desserts including cheesecakes and ice creams, plus some tempting treats like ever-popular cupcakes and brownies.

Simple Swaps for Healthier Eating:

- Swap white rice for brown; white pasta for wholewheat

- Substitute white bread with wholemeal/ wholegrain

- Opt for wholegrain or oat-based breakfast cereals

- Eat more beans, pulses and wholegrains; try ones like quinoa, spelt and farro

- Switch to unrefined sugar or natural sweeteners like honey; reduce the amount you use

- Choose healthier snacks like fresh or dried fruit, mixed seeds, unsalted nuts, low-fat yogurt, crispbreads, fresh vegetable sticks, fruit scones, etc

- Use unsaturated oils for cooking like rapeseed, olive and sunflower oils

- Use salt sparingly (or not at all) when cooking and serving food; instead season foods with herbs, spices, citrus zest, chillies, garlic, mustard, etc

- Shop seasonally to get maximum flavour and nutrients from food

Superfoods

Some foods are thought to have superfood status, providing more nutrients in one serving than other fruits and vegetables. Superfoods that pack a powerful nutritional punch include avocados, bananas, blueberries, broccoli, garlic, kale, nuts, quinoa, spinach, tomatoes, wild salmon and others, so try and include some of these superpower foods in your diet if you can.

BREAKFAST

POACHED EGGS & KALE WITH WHOLEMEAL SOURDOUGH

Serves: 4   **Prep: 20 mins**   **Cook: 15–17 mins**

Ingredients

4 eggs

100 g/3½ oz kale, chopped

4 large slices of wholemeal sourdough bread

2 garlic cloves, halved

2 tbsp olive oil

1 tsp dried red chilli flakes

Method

1 Bring a shallow saucepan of water to a gentle simmer. Crack an egg into a small bowl, then slide the egg into the water, lowering the bowl as close to the water as possible. Using a large spoon, gently fold any stray strands of white around the yolk. Repeat with the other eggs.

2 Cook for 2–3 minutes, or until set to your liking, then remove with a slotted spoon. Place the eggs in a small bowl of warm water so they can sit until needed.

3 Bring a saucepan of water to the boil and add the kale. Simmer for 3–4 minutes, or until the kale is just cooked but still retains a little crunch. Drain and set aside.

4 Meanwhile, toast the bread. Place the toast on four plates, then rub each slice with the garlic and drizzle with the olive oil. Top the toast with the blanched kale and a poached egg. Finally sprinkle over chilli flakes. Serve immediately.

★ Variation

Swap the kale for mashed avocado. Slice two ripe avocados and roughly mash in a bowl. Stir in the juice from half a lime and a teaspoon of paprika. Serve on the bread with the eggs.

HEALTHY BREAKFAST FRITTATA

Serves: 4   **Prep: 15 mins**   **Cook: 20 mins**

Ingredients

250 g/9 oz baby new potatoes, unpeeled and sliced

2 tbsp virgin olive oil

4 spring onions, thinly sliced

1 courgette, thinly sliced

115 g/4 oz baby spinach, de-stalked

¼ tsp smoked hot paprika

6 eggs

salt and pepper (optional)

Method

1 Bring a saucepan of water to the boil, add the potatoes and cook for 5 minutes, or until just tender, then drain well.

2 Meanwhile, heat 1 tablespoon of oil in a large ovenproof frying pan over a medium heat. Add the spring onions, courgette and potatoes and fry, stirring and turning the vegetables, for 5 minutes, or until just beginning to brown.

3 Add the spinach and paprika and cook, stirring, for 1–2 minutes, or until the spinach leaves have just wilted.

4 Preheat the grill to medium–hot. Crack the eggs into a bowl and season with salt and pepper, if using. Beat lightly with a fork until evenly mixed. Pour a little extra oil into the pan if needed, then pour in the eggs and cook for 5–6 minutes, or until they are almost set and the underside of the frittata is golden brown.

5 Grill the frittata for 3–4 minutes, or until the top is browned and the eggs are set. Cut into wedges and serve.

EGG WHITE OMELETTE WITH SPICY THREE-BEAN FILLING

Serves: 1   **Prep: 10 mins**   **Cook: 10 mins**

Ingredients

4 egg whites

¼ tsp salt

1 tbsp water

2 tsp oil from a jar of semi-dried tomatoes

2 spring onions, finely chopped

85 g/3 oz cooked mixed beans, rinsed

40 g/1½ oz frozen sweetcorn, thawed

50 ml/1¾ fl oz hot tomato salsa

3 semi-dried tomatoes in oil, drained and chopped

½ tsp smoked paprika

2 tbsp chopped fresh coriander

5 sprays cooking oil spray

Method

1 Put the egg whites into a bowl with the salt and water and beat together.

2 Place the oil in a small frying pan over a medium heat. Add the spring onion and fry for 1 minute, until soft.

3 Add the beans and sweetcorn to the pan with the tomato salsa, tomatoes and paprika. Cook for a few minutes, then stir in half of the coriander. Set the mixture aside and keep warm.

4 Spray a separate small frying pan with the cooking oil spray and heat over a high heat until very hot. Pour in the egg white mixture and cook, making sure that the egg cooks evenly. When the underside of the omelette is golden and the top is cooked but still moist, spoon the bean filling over the top then sprinkle over the remaining coriander.

5 Tip the pan gently to one side, fold the omelette in half and slide out onto a warmed serving plate. Serve immediately.

SHAKSHUKA EGGS WITH SPICY TOMATO SAUCE

Serves: 4　　　　**Prep: 10 mins**　　　　**Cook: 35 mins**

Ingredients

1 tsp cumin seeds

1 tsp coriander seeds

2 tsp olive oil

1 onion, finely chopped

600 g/1 lb 5 oz canned plum tomatoes

40 g/1½ oz chilli pesto

¼ tsp saffron

¼ tsp cayenne pepper

½ tsp salt

1 tsp pepper

3 tbsp chopped fresh coriander

4 large eggs

Method

1 Crush the cumin seeds and coriander seeds. Place a non-stick frying pan over a medium heat and add the seeds to the pan. Stir for 1 minute, or until their aromas are released.

2 Reduce the heat to medium–low, add the oil and heat. Add the onion and cook, stirring occasionally, for 5 minutes, or until the onion is soft and just turning slightly golden.

3 Add the tomatoes, breaking up any large ones, pesto, saffron, cayenne pepper, salt and pepper. Stir well, bring to a simmer and cook for 15 minutes, adding a little hot water towards the end if the pan looks too dry (but you don't want the sauce to be too runny). Stir in half of the fresh coriander.

4 Make four wells in the sauce and break an egg into each one. Cover the pan and cook over a low heat for 10 minutes, or until the egg whites are set but the yolks are still runny. Sprinkle the remaining fresh coriander over the top and serve immediately.

SPINACH & NUTMEG BAKED EGGS

Serves: 4

Prep: 20 mins, plus cooling

Cook: 20–30 mins

Ingredients

1 tbsp olive oil, for brushing

1 tbsp olive oil, for frying

4 shallots, finely chopped

3 garlic cloves, sliced

100 g/3½ oz baby spinach

8 eggs

½ tsp ground nutmeg

salt and pepper (optional)

Method

1 Preheat the oven to 180°C/350°F/Gas Mark 4. Lightly brush the insides of four 200 ml/7 fl oz ramekins with olive oil.

2 Heat the olive oil in a frying pan. Once hot, add the shallots and garlic and fry over a medium heat for 3–4 minutes, or until soft. Add the baby spinach and stir for 2–3 minutes, or until just wilted. Season with salt and pepper, if using.

3 Spoon the spinach mixture into the bottom of the prepared ramekins and crack two eggs into each. Sprinkle over the nutmeg and place the ramekins in a roasting tin. Fill the roasting tin with boiling water until the water reaches halfway up the ramekins – this creates a steamy environment for the eggs so there is no chance of them drying out.

4 Carefully transfer the roasting tin to the preheated oven for 15–20 minutes. Leave the ramekins to cool slightly then serve immediately.

BREAKFAST BURRITO

Serves: 1   **Prep: 5 mins**   **Cook: 5 mins**

Ingredients

2 egg whites

pinch of salt

½ tsp pepper

1 spring onion, thinly sliced

1 spray vegetable oil spray

30 g/1 oz red or green pepper, deseeded and diced

2 tbsp canned black beans, drained and rinsed

1 wholemeal flour tortilla, warmed

15 g/½ oz crumbled feta cheese

2 tbsp salsa

1 tsp finely chopped fresh coriander, plus extra leaves to garnish

Method

1 In a small bowl, combine the egg whites, salt, pepper and spring onion and stir well.

2 Spray a non-stick frying pan with vegetable oil spray and place it over a medium–high heat. Add the red pepper and cook, stirring, for about 3 minutes or until it begins to soften. Reduce the heat to medium, pour in the egg mixture and cook, stirring often, for a further 1–2 minutes or until the egg sets.

3 Put the beans in a microwave-safe bowl and microwave on High for about 1 minute or until heated through.

4 Spoon the cooked egg mixture onto the tortilla. Top with the beans, cheese, salsa and coriander Serve immediately, garnished with whole coriander leaves.

BAKED MUSHROOMS WITH HERB RICOTTA

Serves: 4 **Prep: 10 mins** **Cook: 15–20 mins**

Ingredients

4 large flat mushrooms

1 tbsp olive oil

shallot, roughly chopped

25 g/1 oz fresh flat-leaf parsley

tbsp snipped fresh chives

140 g/5 oz ricotta cheese

salt and pepper (optional)

Method

1 Preheat the oven to 200°C/400°F/Gas Mark 6. Remove the stalks from the mushrooms and set aside. Place the mushrooms in a shallow baking dish and brush with the oil.

2 Put the mushroom stalks, shallot, parsley and chives in a food processor and blend until finely chopped. Season to taste with salt and pepper, if using.

3 Place the chopped ingredients in a large bowl with the ricotta and stir to mix evenly.

4 Spoon the herb ricotta onto the top of the mushrooms. Bake in the preheated oven for 15–20 minutes, or until tender and bubbling. Serve immediately.

BREAKFAST

COURGETTE FRITTERS

Serves: 5   **Prep: 20 mins**   **Cook: 40 mins**

Ingredients

85 g/3 oz brown rice flour
1 tsp baking powder
2 eggs, beaten
200 ml/7 fl oz milk
250 g/9 oz courgettes
2 tbsp fresh thyme leaves
1 tbsp virgin olive oil
salt and pepper (optional)

Method

1. Sift the flour and baking powder into a large bowl, then tip the remaining bran in the sieve into the bowl. Make a well in the centre. Pour the eggs into the well and, using a wooden spoon, gradually draw in the flour. Slowly pour in the milk, stirring continuously to form a thick batter.

2. Meanwhile, place kitchen paper on a plate and grate the courgettes over it so it absorbs some of the juices. Pat the courgettes dry, then add them and the thyme to the batter, season with salt and pepper, if using, and mix well.

3. Heat the oil in a frying pan over a medium–high heat. Drop tablespoons of the batter into the pan, leaving a little space between them. Cook in batches for 3–4 minutes on each side, or until golden brown.

4. Line a baking sheet with kitchen paper. Transfer the fritters to the baking sheet using a slotted spoon and let them drain well. Remove the kitchen paper and keep each batch warm while you make the rest. Allow five fritters per person and serve immediately.

BREAKFAST

THREE HERB & RICOTTA OMELETTE

Serves: 2 **Prep: 15 mins** **Cook: 8 mins**

Ingredients

4 large eggs

2 tbsp finely snipped fresh chives

2 tbsp finely chopped fresh basil

2 tbsp finely chopped fresh parsley

100 g/3½ oz ricotta cheese, crumbled

2 tbsp olive oil

salt and pepper (optional)

Method

1 Crack the eggs into a small mixing bowl and lightly beat with a fork. Stir the herbs and ricotta into the bowl and season with salt and pepper, if using.

2 Heat the olive oil in a non-stick frying pan over a high heat until hot. Pour in the egg mixture and, using a spatula, draw the outside edges (which will cook more quickly) towards the gooey centre. Allow any liquid mixture to move into the gaps. Continue with this action for about 4–5 minutes. The omelette will continue to cook once the pan is removed from the heat.

3 Cut the omelette in half and divide between two plates. Fold in half and serve immediately.

CRANBERRY & SEED MUESLI

Serves: 6

Prep: 5 mins, plus soaking

Cook: No cooking

Ingredients

175 g/6 oz jumbo porridge oats

40 g/1½ oz rye flakes

40 g/1½ oz whole unblanched almonds, roughly chopped

40 g/1½ oz dried cranberries

2 tbsp sunflower seeds

2 tbsp pumpkin seeds

2 tbsp golden linseeds

2 crisp eating apples

400 ml/14 fl oz apple juice

Method

1 Place the oats, rye flakes, almonds, cranberries, sunflower seeds, pumpkin seeds and linseeds in a large bowl and stir well.

2 Core and roughly grate the apples and stir thoroughly into the dry ingredients.

3 Stir in the apple juice, cover, and leave to soak for about an hour, or refrigerate overnight.

4 To serve, spoon the mixture into six serving bowls.

BARLEY PORRIDGE WITH GRILLED FRUITS

Serves: 4   **Prep: 15 mins**   **Cook: 10-15 mins**

Ingredients

85 g/3 oz barley flakes

85 g/3 oz porridge oats

350 ml/12 fl oz cold water

750 ml/1¼ pints
unsweetened almond milk

4 tsp maca

2 peaches, halved, stoned
and sliced

1 papaya, halved,
deseeded, peeled and
sliced

4 tsp runny honey

½ tsp ground cinnamon

2 tsp runny honey, to serve

Method

1 Put the barley flakes, porridge oats, water and almond milk in a saucepan. Bring to the boil over a medium-high heat, then reduce the heat to medium and simmer for 5-10 minutes, stirring often, until soft and thickened. Stir in the maca.

2 Meanwhile, preheat the grill to medium-high. Line the grill rack with foil, then lay the peaches and papaya on top, drizzle with the honey and sprinkle with the cinnamon. Grill for 3-4 minutes, or until hot and just beginning to caramelize.

3 Spoon the porridge into bowls, top with the hot peaches and papaya and drizzle with the honey before serving.

CITRUS FRUIT REFRESHER

Serves: 4   **Prep: 20 mins**   **Cook: No cooking**

Ingredients

1 ruby grapefruit

1 pink grapefruit

2 oranges

1 honeydew melon, halved, deseeded, peeled and cut into chunks

finely grated zest and juice of 1 lime

25 g/1 oz fresh mint, finely shredded

2 tbsp runny honey

Method

1. Cut the peel and pith away from the grapefruits and oranges with a small serrated knife. Hold one of the fruits above a bowl and cut between the membranes to release the segments. Squeeze the juice from the membranes into the bowl. Continue until the fruits have all been segmented into the bowl.

2. Add the melon, lime zest and juice and half the mint. Drizzle over the honey, then gently stir with a large spoon. Decorate with the remaining mint and serve.

BREAKFAST

CRUNCHY GREEK YOGURT MELON POTS

Serves: 4

Prep: 15 mins, plus chilling

Cook: No cooking

Ingredients

500 g/1 lb 2oz fat-free Greek-style yogurt

1 tsp vanilla extract

275 g/9¾ oz cantaloupe melon, cut into 1-cm/ ½-inch cubes

350 g/12 oz watermelon, cut into 1-cm/½-inch cubes

1 tbsp sunflower seeds

1 tbsp pumpkin seeds

2 tbsp chopped almonds

60 g/2¼ oz ready-made oat granola

Method

1 Beat together the yogurt and vanilla extract. Set half of the yogurt mixture aside. Divide the remaining yogurt mixture between four small glasses or serving dishes.

2 Spoon the cantaloupe melon and the watermelon evenly over the yogurt. Add the remaining yogurt over the top.

3 Mix the seeds, almonds and granola together in a small bowl. Spoon the seed mixture evenly over each yogurt pot. Chill for 30 minutes before serving.

BREAKFAST

VANILLA & BERRY OVERNIGHT PORRIDGE

Serves: 2

Prep: 5 mins,
plus chilling

Cook: No cooking

Ingredients

50 g/1¾ oz rolled oats

150 ml/5 fl oz unsweetened almond milk

½ tsp vanilla extract

2 tsp runny honey

4 tbsp low-fat vanilla yogurt

35 g/1¼ oz blueberries

40 g/1½ oz sliced strawberries

1 tbsp toasted flaked almonds

Method

1 Place the oats in a serving bowl. Pour over the almond milk and stir in the vanilla extract and honey. Cover and refrigerate for at least 4 hours or overnight.

2 Remove the mixture from the refrigerator, add the yogurt and stir well. Divide between two bowls, top with the blueberries, strawberries and almonds and serve immediately.

BREAKFAST

SPICED QUINOA PORRIDGE

Serves: 2　　　　**Prep: 10 mins**　　　　**Cook: 35 mins**

Ingredients

100 g/3½ oz white quinoa

½ tsp ground cinnamon

⅛ tsp ground nutmeg

¼ tsp ground ginger

¼ tsp salt

350 ml/12 fl oz skimmed milk

125 ml/4 fl oz water

2 tbsp sultanas

1 tbsp maple syrup

½ tsp vanilla extract

Method

1 Heat a large, heavy-based saucepan over a medium heat and add the quinoa and cinnamon. Cook, stirring constantly, for about 3 minutes, or until fragrant and lightly toasted. Stir in the nutmeg, ginger and salt.

2 Pour in the milk and water and stir in the sultanas, maple syrup and vanilla extract. Bring to the boil, then reduce the heat to low and simmer for about 25 minutes, stirring several times, until the porridge is thick and the grains are tender. Add more water if the liquid dries up before the grains are tender.

3 Serve the porridge immediately.

BREAKFAST

CHIA SEED & PISTACHIO BREAKFAST PUDDING

Serves: 4   **Prep: 5 mins,** plus chilling   **Cook: No cooking**

Ingredients

225 ml/8 fl oz unsweetened almond milk

225 ml/8 fl oz natural low-fat yogurt

2 tbsp pure maple syrup

1½ tsp vanilla extract

pinch of salt

35 g/1¼ oz chia seeds

225 g/8 oz strawberries, sliced

40 g/1½ oz toasted pistachio nuts, chopped

maple syrup, for drizzling (optional)

Method

1 Put the almond milk, yogurt, maple syrup, vanilla extract and salt into a medium-sized bowl and stir to combine.

2 Stir in the chia seeds and leave to stand for about 30 minutes at room temperature. Stir the mixture well to make sure the seeds are well incorporated, then cover and chill in the refrigerator for at least 8 hours or overnight.

3 To serve, spoon the pudding into serving bowls and top with the strawberries, nuts and a drizzle of maple syrup, if using.

LOW-FAT MOZZARELLA BREAKFAST MUFFIN

Serves: 1　　　　**Prep: 10 mins**　　　　**Cook: 5 mins**

Ingredients

1 large egg

1 tbsp skimmed milk

2 sprays light cooking oil spray

1 wholegrain English muffin

30 g/1 oz reduced-fat soft mozzarella cheese, sliced

Tomato relish

1 ripe tomato, weighing about 90 g/3¼ oz

¼ ready-roasted red pepper from a jar, drained and chopped

2 tsp red pesto

¼ tsp pepper

¼ tsp smoked paprika

Method

1　To make the relish, peel, halve and deseed the tomato and roughly chop the flesh. Place the tomato in a small bowl with the red pepper, pesto, pepper and paprika and stir well to combine. If you prefer the relish warm, heat in the microwave for 1 minute on Medium–Low just before serving.

2　Beat the egg with the milk in a small bowl. Place a small frying pan over a medium heat and spray in the cooking oil spray. Cook the egg mixture, stirring occasionally, until scrambled but not too dry. Remove from the heat. Meanwhile, halve and toast the muffin.

3　As soon as the egg and muffin are ready, cover the bottom half of the muffin with the cheese slices, spread with half the tomato relish and spoon the egg on top. Spoon the remaining relish over the egg and top with the remaining muffin half. Serve immediately.

FRUITY GRANOLA CUPS

Serves: 2   **Prep: 25 mins**   **Cook: 35 mins**

Ingredients

115 g/4 oz medium oatmeal

85 g/3 oz porridge oats

40 g/1½ oz unblanched almonds, roughly chopped

2 tbsp pumpkin seeds

2 tbsp sunflower seeds

2 tbsp linseeds, coarsely ground

½ tsp ground cinnamon

3 tbsp maple syrup

1 tbsp olive oil

25 g/1 oz goji berries

To serve

115 g/4 oz granola

juice of 1 orange

115 g/4 oz Greek-style natural yogurt

1 dessert apple, cored and coarsely grated

115 g/4 oz strawberries, hulled and sliced

40 g/1½ oz blueberries

Method

1 Preheat the oven to 160°C/325°F/Gas Mark 3. Put the oatmeal, porridge oats and almonds in a bowl. Stir in the pumpkin seeds, sunflower seeds and linseeds, then the cinnamon, maple syrup and oil.

2 Tip the granola into a roasting tin, then spread into an even layer. Bake for 30–35 minutes, or until golden brown all over, stirring every 5–10 minutes and mixing any browner granola from the edges of the tin into the centre after 15 minutes.

3 Stir in the goji berries, then leave to cool. Pack into an airtight container and store in the refrigerator for up to five days.

4 When ready to serve, spoon the granola into two glasses or bowls, keeping a little back for the top Moisten with the orange juice. Mix the yogurt with the apple, spoon over the granola, top with the strawberries and blueberries and sprinkle

BREAKFAST POWER BALLS

Serves: 4

Prep: 15 mins, plus chilling

Cook: No cooking

Ingredients

70 g/2½ oz ground almonds

70 g/2½ oz cashew nuts, finely chopped

3 tbsp ground linseeds

40 g/1½ oz raw cacao

100 g/3½ oz ready-to-eat dried apricots, finely chopped

1 tbsp maple syrup

½ tsp vanilla extract

1 large ripe dessert pear, cored and cut into thin slices

2 oranges, cut into segments

Method

1 Place the almonds, half of the cashew nuts, the linseeds, cacao, apricots, maple syrup and vanilla extract in a mixing bowl. Mix thoroughly until well combined – add a few drops of cold water if the mixture does not come together easily. Divide the mixture into 16 pieces and roll each piece into a ball.

2 Put the remaining cashew nuts into a shallow bowl. Dip each ball into the nuts and turn until lightly coated. Transfer to an airtight container and refrigerate for several hours before eating.

3 To serve, arrange the pear slices and orange segments on four serving plates. Place four balls on each plate and serve immediately.

BUCKWHEAT PANCAKES WITH RASPBERRY SAUCE

Serves: 4

Prep: 5 mins, plus resting

Cook: 15 mins

Ingredients

1 egg
275 ml/9 fl oz skimmed milk
½ tsp salt
2 tsp sunflower oil
60 g/2¼ oz wholemeal flour
60 g/2¼ oz buckwheat flour
32 sprays cooking oil spray

Raspberry sauce
250 g/9 oz raspberries
2 tbsp water
2 tbsp stevia granules

Method

1 Beat the egg in a mixing bowl, then stir in the milk, salt and oil and beat until well combined. Put the wholemeal flour and buckwheat flour into a separate bowl and mix together. Stir the milk mixture into the flour mixture and beat until smooth. Cover and leave the batter to rest for up to 30 minutes.

2 Meanwhile, to make the raspberry sauce, gently heat the raspberries with the water in a saucepan until the juices run. Stir in the stevia until the granules are completely dissolved. Push the mixture through a fine sieve to remove any pips. Leave to cool completely.

3 When ready to make the pancakes, place a small frying pan over a high heat and add 4 sprays of cooking oil. When the oil is very hot, spoon one eighth of the batter into the pan and swirl around to coat the base of the pan evenly. Cook until the underside of the pancake is nicely golden – this will take only a minute or so. Turn the pancake over with a large spatula and cook until golden on the other side. Remove and keep the pancake warm while you cook the remaining pancakes, spraying the pan each time with up to 4 sprays of oil, or as necessary.

4 Serve the pancakes on four warmed plates and pour over the raspberry sauce.

BREAKFAST

WHOLEMEAL CRÊPES

Serves: 6

Prep: 25 mins **Cook: 25 mins**

Ingredients

Mushroom filling

1 tbsp olive oil

1 garlic clove, finely chopped

1 shallot, finely chopped

675 g/1 lb 8oz button mushrooms, sliced

½ tsp salt

½ tsp pepper

Crêpes

150 g/5½ oz wholemeal flour

2 large eggs

300 ml/10 fl oz skimmed milk

¼ tsp salt

2 tbsp unsalted butter, melted

2 sprays of vegetable oil spray

115 g/4 oz reduced-fat soured cream, to serve

3 tbsp snipped chives, to garnish

Method

1 To make the mushroom filling, heat the oil in a large frying pan over a medium–high heat. Add the garlic and shallot and cook for about 5 minutes until soft. Add the mushrooms and continue to cook for about 5 minutes, stirring, until they soften. Season with the salt and pepper. Remove from the heat and keep warm.

2 To make the crêpes, place the flour, eggs, milk, salt and butter in a medium bowl. Beat together with an electric whisk.

3 Coat a large non-stick frying pan with vegetable oil spray and place it over a medium heat. When the frying pan is hot, ladle the crêpe mixture, about 60 ml/2 fl oz at a time, into the hot frying pan. Tilt the pan to spread the mixture into a thin, even round about 15 cm/6 inches in diameter. Cook for about 1 minute until the crêpe begins to colour lightly underneath. Using a palette knife, gently flip the crêpe over and cook for a further 45 seconds on the other side, or until it is lightly coloured. Stack the crêpes as they are cooked and keep warm.

4 When all of the crêpes are cooked, spoon 2–3 tbsp of the filling onto each crêpe and fold in half twice. Serve with a dollop of soured cream and garnish with chives.

BREAKFAST

SPELT BREAKFAST ROLLS WITH SPICED FIG CONSERVE

**Makes: 16 rolls
& 500 g jar of conserve**

Prep: 45 mins,
plus rising & cooling

Cook: 50 mins

Ingredients

500 g/1 lb 2oz wholemeal
spelt plain flour

1 tbsp dark
muscovado sugar

1 tsp sea salt

2 tsp easy-blend
dried yeast

2 tbsp sesame seeds

2 tbsp sunflower seeds

2 tbsp linseeds

2 tbsp virgin olive oil

300-350 ml/10-12 fl oz warm
water

10 g/¼ oz wholemeal spelt
plain flour, for dusting

1 tbsp virgin olive oil,
for greasing

1 tsp milk,
for glazing

Spiced fig conserve

225 g/8 oz dried figs, diced

3 small dessert apples,
peeled, quartered, cored
and diced

finely grated zest and juice
of 1 orange

1 tbsp light
muscovado sugar

¼ tsp ground mixed spice

250 ml/9 fl oz water

Method

1 Put the flour, dark muscovado sugar and salt in
a bowl and mix well. Stir in the yeast and most of
the sesame seeds, sunflower seeds and linseeds,
reserving the rest for sprinkling. Add the oil, then
gradually mix in enough warm water to create a
soft dough, at first using a wooden spoon, then
squeezing together with your hands.

2 Dust a work surface with the spelt flour, then
knead the dough for 5 minutes. Return it to the
bowl, cover with lightly oiled clingfilm and leave
it to rise overnight in the refrigerator.

3 Meanwhile, to make the spiced fig conserve, put
the dried figs, apples, orange zest and juice, light
muscovado sugar, mixed spice and water in a
saucepan. Cover and simmer over a medium
heat, stirring from time to time, for 30 minutes, or
until thick. Leave to cool. Sterilise a 500 g/
1 lb 2 oz jar, then spoon in the conserve, cover
and leave until completely cold. Chill in the
refrigerator, where it will keep for up to 10 days.

4 Line two baking sheets with baking paper.
Dust a work surface with more of the spelt flour.
Knead the dough briefly, then cut it into 16
equal pieces.

BREAKFAST

- Roll each piece into a ball, put one ball in the centre of each baking sheet, then arrange the others around it, leaving a little space between them. Cover each sheet with lightly oiled clingfilm and leave to rise in a warm place for 40–50 minutes.

- Preheat the oven to 220°C/425°F/Gas Mark 7. Remove the clingfilm, brush the rolls with the milk and sprinkle with the remaining seeds. Bake for 15 minutes, or until the rolls are browned and sound hollow when tapped underneath. Serve with butter and the conserve.

JUMBO CARROT CAKE BISCUITS

Makes: 12   **Prep: 30 mins**   **Cook: 20 mins**

Ingredients

100 g/3½ oz linseeds

85 g/3 oz wholemeal plain flour

70 g/2½ oz porridge oats

1 tsp baking powder

1 tsp ground ginger

2 tsp ground cinnamon

85 g/3 oz dried apricots, finely chopped

1 dessert apple, cored and coarsely grated

1 carrot, finely grated

40 g/1½ oz pecan nuts

3 tbsp coconut oil

125 ml/4 fl oz maple syrup

grated zest of ½ orange, plus 3 tbsp juice

4 tbsp dried coconut shavings

Method

1 Preheat the oven to 180°C/350°F/Gas Mark 4 and line two baking sheets with baking paper.

2 Put the linseeds in a blender and process to a fine powder, then tip into a mixing bowl. Add the flour, oats and baking powder, then the ginger and cinnamon, and stir well. Add the dried apricots, apple and carrot. Roughly chop the pecan nuts and stir into the mixture.

3 Warm the coconut oil in a small saucepan (or in the microwave for 30 seconds) until just liquid. Remove from the heat, then stir in the maple syrup and orange zest and juice. Pour this into the carrot mixture and stir together until you have a soft dough.

4 Spoon 12 mounds of the mixture onto the prepared baking sheets, then flatten them into thick 7.5-cm/3-inch diameter rounds. Sprinkle with the coconut shavings, then bake for 15–18 minutes, or until browned.

5 Serve warm or leave to cool, then pack into a plastic container and store in the refrigerator for up to three days.

BREAKFAST

HEALTHY FRENCH TOAST

Serves: 4 **Prep: 20 mins** **Cook: 12–17 mins**

Ingredients

60 g/2¼ oz pecan nuts, roughly chopped

2 eggs

4 ripe bananas, sliced

½ tsp vanilla extract

½ tsp ground cinnamon

4 slices thick wholemeal bread

1 tbsp olive oil

½ tsp ground cinnamon, to sprinkle

Method

1 Place the pecans in a small, dry frying pan and toast over a medium heat for 3–4 minutes, tossing regularly until just toasted. Set aside.

2 Place the eggs, 2 bananas, vanilla extract and cinnamon in a blender and whizz for 1–2 minutes, or until the consistency is smooth and thick.

3 Pour the mixture into a medium, shallow dish. Place two slices of bread in the mixture and, working quickly, gently press the bread into the liquid, allowing it to soak up the mixture. Turn the slices over and repeat.

4 Meanwhile, heat half of the olive oil in a large, non-stick frying pan over a medium–high heat. Using a spatula, remove the soaked bread from the banana mixture and place in the frying pan. Cook for 2–3 minutes on each side before removing from the pan. Repeat the process for the remaining slices, adding the remaining olive oil if needed.

5 Serve the banana bread immediately, with a sprinkling of cinnamon and the toasted pecans and remaining sliced bananas on top.

BREAKFAST

SUPER-POWERED MANGO JUICE

Serves: 1   **Prep: 15–20 mins**   **Cook: No cooking**

Ingredients

2 clementines, zest and a little pith removed

1 mango, stoned and peeled

2 apples, peeled, halved and cored

small handful of ice, to serve (optional)

chilled water, to taste

1 tsp clear honey

Method

1 Feed the clementines, mango and apples through a juicer.

2 Half-fill a glass with ice, if using. Pour in the juice, top up with water to taste, stir in the honey and serve immediately.

MUESLI MOTIVATOR JUICE

Serves: 1 **Prep: 15 mins** **Cook: No cooking**

Ingredients

20 g/¾ oz porridge oats

30 g/1 oz flaked almonds

½ ruby red grapefruit, zest
and a little pith removed,
deseeded and roughly
chopped

150 g/5½ oz raspberries

juice of 2 oranges

125 ml/4 fl oz chilled water

Method

1 Put the porridge oats and almonds in a blender
and whizz until finely ground.

2 Add the grapefruit, raspberries, orange juice and
water and whizz until smooth.

3 Pour into a glass and serve.

PROTEIN BERRY WHIP SMOOTHIE

Serves: 4　　　　**Prep: 10–15 mins**　　　　**Cook: No cooking**

Ingredients

125 g/4½ oz frozen sliced strawberries

125 g/4½ oz frozen blueberries

40 g/1½ oz Brazil nuts, chopped

40 g/1½ oz cashew nut pieces

25 g/1 oz porridge oats

450 ml/15 fl oz almond milk

2 tbsp maple syrup

Method

1 Place the strawberries, blueberries, Brazil nuts and cashew nut pieces in a blender. Sprinkle over the oats, then pour in half the almond milk Blend until smooth.

2 Add the remaining milk and the maple syrup, and blend again until smooth.

3 Pour into four glasses and serve immediately with spoons. As the drink stands, the blueberries will almost set the liquid, but as soon as you stir it, it will turn to liquid again.

SUPER SMOOTHIE

Serves: 1   **Prep: 10–15 mins**   **Cook: No cooking**

Ingredients

30 g/1 oz spinach

250 ml/9 fl oz cooled liquorice tea

½ avocado, stoned and flesh scooped from skin

1 frozen banana

1 tsp chia seeds

½ tsp chia seeds, to garnish

Method

1 Blend the spinach and liquorice tea in a blender until smooth.

2 Chop the avocado, add it to the blender with the banana and chia seeds, and blend until smooth and creamy. Serve immediately, garnished with a sprinkle of chia seeds.

★ Variation

Try an avocado and grape smoothie instead. Prepare the avocado in the same way and blend with 115 g/4 oz green seedless grapes and the juice from half an orange. Add a small handful of crushed ice and blend again. Pour in a glass, fill up with water to taste, and serve the smoothie immediately.

SNACKS & SIDES

ROSEMARY, SEA SALT & SESAME POPCORN

Serves: 4   **Prep: 10–15 mins**   **Cook: 6–8 mins**

Ingredients

40 g/1½ oz sesame seeds

2 tbsp olive oil

2 rosemary stems,
torn into large pieces

200 g/7 oz popping corn

1 tsp sea salt

2 tbsp balsamic vinegar,
or to taste

Method

1 Add the sesame seeds to a large frying pan with
1 teaspoon of the oil, cover and cook over a
medium heat for 2–3 minutes, shaking the pan
from time to time, until the seeds are toasted
golden brown and beginning to pop. Scoop out
of the pan into a bowl and wipe out the pan
with a piece of kitchen paper.

2 Add the remaining oil and the rosemary to the
pan and heat gently. Add the corn, cover with
the lid and cook over a medium heat for 3–4
minutes, shaking the pan, until all the popcorn
has popped. Remove from the heat and sprinkle
with the toasted sesame seeds and season with
the salt and vinegar. Discard the rosemary just
before eating.

★ Variation

Make popcorn bars. Grease a 23 x 33-cm/9 x
13-inch Swiss roll tin. Line with baking paper. Use
25 g/1 oz of popping corn and prepare as per
the packet instructions. Melt 250 g/9 oz of dark
chocolate and pour into the prepared tin. Mix
the popcorn with a handful of finely chopped
dried apricots, raisins and pecan nuts and
scatter over the melted chocolate. Chill in the
refrigerator for 30 minutes, or until set.

APPLE & CINNAMON CRISPS

Serves: 4

Prep: 20–25 mins, plus cooling

Cook: 1hr 30 mins - 2hrs

Ingredients

1 litre/1¾ pints water

1 tbsp sea salt

3 dessert apples, such as Braeburn or Gala

¼ tsp ground cinnamon

Method

1 Preheat the oven to 110°C/225°F/Gas Mark ¼. Put the water and salt into a large mixing bowl and stir until the salt has dissolved.

2 Very thinly slice the apples, one at a time, with a sharp knife or mandolin, leaving the skin on and the core still in place, but removing any pips. Add each apple slice to the water. Turn to coat in the salt water, which will help prevent discoloration.

3 Drain the apple slices in a colander, then lightly pat dry with a clean tea towel. Arrange in a thin layer on a large cooking or roasting rack. Place this in the oven so that the heat can circulate under the slices as well as over the tops.

4 Bake for 1½–2 hours, until the apple slices are dry and crisp. Loosen with a palette knife and transfer to a large plate or chopping board, then sprinkle with cinnamon. Leave to cool completely, then serve or pack into a plastic container, seal and keep in the refrigerator for up to 2 days.

HOME-MADE SPICED PEANUT BUTTER

Serves: 8   **Prep: 15 mins**   **Cook: No cooking**

Ingredients

200 g/7 oz unsalted peanuts
½ tsp salt
½ tsp paprika
½ tbsp groundnut oil

Method

1 Place the nuts and salt in the bowl of a small food processor or chopper. Pulse, switching off every 20 seconds so that the machine does not overheat. Keep pulsing until the nuts progress from a crumble to a paste and then to a thick cream consistency.

2 Add the paprika and blend for a further 30 seconds, then drizzle in the oil and blend again.

3 Store the spiced peanut butter in a lidded jar or airtight plastic container in the refrigerator for up to 5 days.

FIG & OAT BITES

Prep: 20–25 mins, plus cooling   **Cook: 20 mins**

Ingredients

450 g/1 lb soft dried figs

3 tbsp coconut oil, at room temperature

½ tsp ground ginger

½ tsp ground cinnamon

juice of 1 large orange

200 g/7 oz rolled oats

1 tbsp chia seeds

Method

1 Preheat the oven to 180°C/350°F/Gas Mark 4. Line a 23-cm/9-inch square baking tin with baking paper.

2 Place the dried figs, coconut oil, ginger and cinnamon in a food processor and pulse until roughly chopped. Add the orange juice and oats and pulse again until the mixture just comes together. If a little dry, add a touch more orange juice; if a little wet, stir through a few more oats. Add the chia seeds and pulse again very briefly.

3 Spoon the mixture into the prepared baking tin. Use the back of a greased spatula to push the mixture to the corners and spread it evenly.

4 Bake in the preheated oven for 20 minutes. Remove from the oven and, using a sharp knife, cut into 25 small squares. Leave to cool completely on a wire rack and then serve.

GOJI, MANGO & PISTACHIO POPCORN SLICES

Makes: 12

Prep: 25 mins,
plus chilling

Cook: 6–8 mins

Ingredients

1 tbsp light olive oil

40 g/1½ oz popping corn

115 g/4 oz crunchy peanut butter

2 tbsp coconut oil

2 tbsp maple syrup

6 tbsp full-fat or semi-skimmed milk

100 g/3½ oz plain chocolate, 70% cocoa solids, broken into pieces

25 g/1 oz goji berries, roughly chopped

25 g/1 oz dried mango slices, finely chopped

25 g/1 oz pistachio nuts, roughly chopped

15 g/½ oz sunflower seeds

15 g/½ oz pumpkin seeds

Method

1 Line a 20-cm/8-inch shallow square cake tin with a sheet of non-stick baking paper.

2 Heat the olive oil in a frying pan, then add the corn, cover with a lid and cook over a medium heat for 3–4 minutes, until all the corn has popped. Transfer to a bowl, discarding any grains that haven't popped, and wipe out the pan with kitchen paper.

3 Add the peanut butter, coconut oil, maple syrup and milk, and heat gently for 2–3 minutes, stirring until smooth. Remove from the heat, add the chocolate and set aside for 4–5 minutes, until the chocolate has melted.

4 Add the popcorn to the chocolate mix and lightly stir together. Tip into the prepared tin, press down flat with the back of a fork, then sprinkle with the goji berries, mango, pistachios, sunflower and pumpkin seeds. Press the topping into the soft chocolate mix, then chill in the refrigerator for 2 hours, until firmly set.

5 Lift the chocolate mixture out of the tin, place on a chopping board, peel away and reserve the paper, then cut the slice into 12 pieces. Pack into a plastic container, layering with the reserved paper. Keep in the refrigerator for up to 4 days.

COCONUT, CACAO & HAZELNUT TRUFFLES

Makes: 20   **Prep: 25 mins**   **Cook: No cooking**

Ingredients

85 g/3 oz unblanched hazelnuts

55 g/2 oz cacao nibs

6 soft dried figs, roughly chopped

25 g/1 oz desiccated coconut

1 tbsp maple syrup

finely grated rind and juice of ½ small orange

1 tbsp cacao nibs, for coating

2 tbsp desiccated coconut, for coating

Method

1 Add the hazelnuts and the 55 g/2 oz cacao nibs to a food processor and process until very finely chopped.

2 Add the figs, the 25 g/1 oz coconut, maple syrup and orange rind and juice to the processor, and process until finely chopped and the mixture has come together in a ball.

3 Scoop the mixture out of the food processor, then cut into 20 even-sized pieces. Roll into small balls in your hands.

4 Finely chop the extra cacao nibs, then mix with the extra coconut on a sheet of non-stick baking paper or a plate. Roll the truffles, one at a time, in the cacao and coconut mixture, then arrange in a small plastic container. Store in the refrigerator for up to 3 days.

FROZEN YOGURT-COATED BERRIES

Serves: 4

Prep: 20–25 mins, plus freezing

Cook: No cooking

Ingredients

225 g/8 oz fat-free Greek-style yogurt

1 tbsp clear honey

¼ tsp vanilla extract

115 g/4 oz blueberries

125 g/4½ oz raspberries

Method

1. Line three baking sheets or trays with non-stick baking paper, checking first that they will fit into your freezer.

2. Place the yogurt, honey and vanilla extract in a medium-sized bowl and stir together. Drop a few blueberries into the yogurt, then use two forks to coat the berries in a thin layer of yogurt. Lift out, one berry at a time, draining off the excess yogurt, and transfer to one of the lined trays.

3. Continue dipping and coating until all the blueberries are on the tray. Repeat with the raspberries. Freeze, uncovered, for 2–3 hours, until frozen hard.

4. Lift the berries from the trays and pack into polythene bags or lidded plastic containers. Seal and freeze for up to 1 month.

5. Remove as many as you need from the freezer and leave to thaw for 10 minutes before serving so that the fruit can soften slightly.

SNACKS & SIDES

WALNUT, PAPRIKA & RICOTTA DIP

Serves: 4

Prep: 10 mins,
plus chilling

Cook: No cooking

Ingredients

25 g/1 oz walnuts, chopped

125 g/4½ oz ricotta cheese

125 g/4½ oz fat-free Greek-style yogurt

1 tsp dried oregano

1 tsp garlic purée

½ tsp salt

1 tsp sweet paprika

Method

1 Place half the walnuts in a food processor or chopper and pulse until a paste forms. Beat together the ricotta, yogurt, pulsed nuts, oregano, garlic, salt and half the paprika in a small bowl until you have a fairly smooth purée.

2 Stir in all but a few of the remaining nuts. Transfer to a serving dish. Cover and chill for 1 hour.

3 Sprinkle over the remaining paprika and walnut pieces and serve.

RED LENTIL & SWEET POTATO PÂTÉ

Serves: 4

Prep: 15 mins, plus chilling

Cook: 35 mins

Ingredients

2 tbsp olive oil

1 small onion, very finely chopped

2 garlic cloves, crushed

1¼ tsp sweet paprika

¼ tsp cayenne pepper

1 tsp pepper

1 sweet potato, about 250 g/9 oz peeled weight, cut into 1-cm/½-inch cubes

150 g/5½ oz red lentils

350 ml/12 fl oz vegetable stock

juice of ½ small orange

¼ cucumber

2 wholemeal pittas

2 large celery sticks, cut into batons

salt (optional)

Method

1 Place a frying pan over a medium–low heat and add half of the oil. Add the onion and cook, stirring occasionally, for about 10 minutes, or until soft and golden.

2 Add the garlic, 1 teaspoon of the paprika, the cayenne pepper and pepper and cook for a further 2 minutes. Add the sweet potato, lentils and stock. Bring to a simmer and cook, uncovered, stirring occasionally, for 20 minutes, or until the potato and lentils are tender. You may need to add a little more liquid towards the end of cooking time if the pan dries out before the vegetables and lentils are cooked.

3 Add the orange juice and salt to taste, if using. Mash the mixture to a smooth consistency, or to your liking, and spoon into a serving bowl. Chill in the refrigerator for 30 minutes, then drizzle with the remaining oil and sprinkle over the remaining paprika.

4 Cut the cucumber into quarters lengthways and remove the seeds with a sharp knife. Cut the cucumber into batons. Lightly toast the pittas and cut each one into six pieces. Serve the pâté with the pitta bread and the cucumber and celery batons.

CANNELLINI DIP WITH CRUDITÉS

Serves: 4

Prep: 10 mins, plus chilling

Cook: No cooking

Ingredients

400 g/14 oz canned cannellini beans, drained and rinsed

2 garlic cloves, crushed

juice of ½ lemon

4 tbsp olive oil

½ tsp salt

1 tsp black pepper

1 tsp smoked paprika

3 tbsp finely chopped fresh flat-leaf parsley

3 carrots, cut into batons

4 small celery sticks, cut into batons

4 radishes, quartered

1 yellow pepper, sliced

Method

1 Place the beans in a food processor or blender with the garlic, lemon juice, oil, salt, pepper and half the paprika. Blend until completely smooth. If you think the dip is a little thick, beat in a little water, 1 teaspoon at a time, until you achieve the desired consistency.

2 Stir the parsley into the dip and spoon into four ramekins. Cover and chill in the refrigerator for 1–2 hours to allow the flavours to mature.

3 Sprinkle the remaining paprika over the dip and place the ramekins on four serving plates. Arrange the vegetables around the ramekins and serve.

CHICKEN & CHEESE STUFFED MINI PEPPERS

Makes: 12   **Prep: 30–35 mins**   **Cook: 15 mins**

Ingredients

1 tbsp olive oil, for oiling

70 g/2½ oz full-fat cream cheese

2 garlic cloves, finely chopped

2 tsp finely chopped fresh rosemary

1 tbsp finely chopped fresh basil

1 tbsp finely chopped fresh parsley

15 g/½ oz finely grated Parmesan cheese

150 g/5½ oz cooked chicken breast, finely chopped

3 spring onions, finely chopped

12 mixed coloured baby peppers, about 350 g/12 oz total weight

salt and pepper (optional)

Method

1 Preheat the oven to 190°C/375°F/Gas Mark 5. Lightly brush a large baking sheet with oil.

2 Put the cream cheese, garlic, rosemary, basil and parsley in a bowl, then add the Parmesan and stir together with a metal spoon.

3 Mix in the chicken and spring onions, then season with a little salt and pepper, if using.

4 Slit each pepper from the tip up to the stalk, leaving the stalk in place, then make a small cu just to the side, so that you can get a teaspoon into the centre of the pepper to scoop out all the seeds.

5 Fill each pepper with some of the chicken mixture, then place on the prepared baking sheet. Cook in the preheated oven for 15 minutes, or until the peppers are soft and light brown in patches.

6 Leave to cool slightly on the baking sheet, then transfer to a serving plate. Serve warm or cold. These peppers are best eaten on the day they are made and should be kept in the refrigerator if serving cold.

GARLIC & HERB PITTA CRISPS

Serves: 4　　　**Prep: 10 mins**　　　**Cook: 10 mins**

Ingredients

4 wholemeal pittas

32 sprays extra virgin olive
oil cooking spray

1 tsp dried chopped garlic

1 tsp Italian seasoning

½ tsp smoked paprika

Method

1. Preheat the oven to 180°C/350°F/Gas Mark 4. Cut each pitta into quarters and then cut each quarter into two triangles. Separate each triangle into two thin halves so you have 64 crisps in total.

2. Put the crisps on two baking sheets. Spray half of the cooking spray to coat all the crisps, then turn them over and sprinkle over the garlic, seasoning and paprika. Spray with the remaining spray.

3. Bake in the preheated oven for 8 minutes, or un lightly crisp (the pittas will become crisper as they cool).

4. Leave to cool before serving.

SNACKS & SIDES

ROASTED KALE CRISPS

Serves: 4   **Prep: 15 mins**   **Cook: 15 mins**

Ingredients

250 g/9 oz kale

2 tbsp olive oil

½ tsp sugar

2 pinches of sea salt

2 tbsp toasted flaked almonds, to garnish

Method

1 Preheat the oven to 150°C/300°F/Gas Mark 2. Remove the thick stems and central rib from the kale (leaving about 125 g/4½ oz trimmed leaves). Rinse and dry very thoroughly with kitchen paper. Tear the leaves into bite-sized pieces and place in a bowl with the oil and sugar, then toss well.

2 Spread about half the leaves in a single layer in a large roasting tin, spaced well apart. Sprinkle with a pinch of sea salt and roast on the bottom rack of the preheated oven for 4 minutes.

3 Stir the leaves, then turn the tray so the back is at the front. Roast for a further 1–2 minutes, until the leaves are crisp and very slightly browned at the edges. Repeat with the remaining leaves and sea salt. Sprinkle the kale crisps with the flaked almonds and serve immediately.

SNACKS & SIDES

CHICKEN, KALE & CHIA SEED BITES

Makes: 16

Prep: 20–25 mins, plus cooling

Cook: 21 mins

Ingredients

2 x 125 -g/4½-oz skinless, boneless chicken breasts

1 garlic clove, finely chopped

55 g/2 oz kale, shredded

115 g/4 oz light cream cheese

grated zest of 1 lemon

2 tsp chia seeds

salt and pepper (optional)

Method

1 Place the chicken breasts in the top of a steamer half-filled with boiling water. Sprinkle with the garlic, season with salt and pepper, if using, cover with a lid and cook over a medium heat for 20 minutes, or until the juices run clear with no trace of pink when the chicken is pierced with a sharp knife.

2 Add the kale to the steamer and cook for 1 minute to soften it slightly.

3 Remove the steamer from the pan and leave to cool, then finely chop the chicken and kale.

4 Mix the cream cheese, lemon zest and chia seeds together, then stir in the chicken and kale. Taste and adjust the seasoning if using.

5 Using two teaspoons, scoop spoonfuls of the mixture onto a plate, scraping off with the second spoon. Roll the mixture into balls, then pack into a plastic container. Seal and store in the refrigerator for up to 2 days.

ROASTED CHICKPEAS & EDAMAME

Serves: 6   **Prep: 5 mins**   **Cook: 30 mins**

Ingredients

200 g/7 oz canned
chickpeas, drained and
rinsed

200 g/7 oz frozen
edamame beans

tbsp soya or light olive oil

1 tsp za'atar

1 tsp pepper

tsp ground cumin seeds

Method

1 Preheat the oven to 190°C/375°F/Gas Mark 5.

2 Toss the chickpeas and edamame in a large
bowl with the oil, za'atar, pepper and cumin
seeds until thoroughly coated. Spread in a
single layer on a baking tray and roast in the
preheated oven for 30 minutes, stirring every 10
minutes, until the chickpeas and beans are light
golden and crunchy.

3 Leave the mixture to cool, then transfer to a bowl
and serve immediately.

SNACKS & SIDES

CHIPOTLE TURKEY CROQUETTES

Serves: 4   **Prep: 35–40 mins**   **Cook: 20–25 mins**

Ingredients

1-2 tbsp olive oil

4 spring onions, quartered

1 small red pepper, deseeded and cut into chunks

1 carrot, coarsely grated

2 tsp fresh thyme leaves

500 g/1 lb fresh turkey breast mince

1 tsp mild paprika

1 small dried chipotle chilli, finely chopped

1 egg

1 tbsp cold water

25 g/1 oz freshly grated Parmesan cheese

55 g/2 oz golden linseeds, finely ground

salt and pepper (optional)

Avocado dip

1 large ripe avocado, halved and stoned

grated zest and juice of 1 lime

2 tbsp fat-free Greek-style yogurt

Method

1 Preheat the oven to 200°C/400°F/Gas Mark 6. Brush a baking sheet with a little of the oil. Finely chop the spring onions and red pepper in a food processor.

2 Add the carrot, thyme and turkey, then sprinkle over the paprika, chilli and a little salt and pepper, if using. Process until it is all evenly mixed together.

3 Scoop out dessertspoons of the mixture onto a chopping board to make 16 oval-shaped mounds, then press them into neater shapes between your hands.

4 Lightly mix the egg, water and a little salt and pepper together in a shallow dish. Mix the Parmesan cheese and linseeds in a separate shallow dish.

5 Dip the croquettes, one at a time, into the egg, lift out with two forks, draining well, then roll in the cheese mixture.

6 Place on the prepared baking sheet. Continue until all the croquettes are coated.

7 Bake in the preheated oven for 20–25 minutes, until golden, turning halfway through cooking and brushing with the remaining oil, if needed.

To check that they are cooked, cut one croquette in half – the juices will run clear with no traces of pink. When the croquettes are almost ready to serve, make the dip. Scoop the avocado from the shell, mash with the lime zest and juice, and mix with the yogurt.

Spoon into a small bowl set on a large plate, then arrange the hot croquettes around the dish and serve immediately.

VIETNAMESE PRAWN RICE ROLLS

Makes: 6   **Prep: 40 mins**   **Cook: No cooking**

Ingredients

40 g/1½ oz vermicelli rice noodles

150 g/5½ oz cooked and chilled tiger prawns

grated zest of 1 lime

55 g/2 oz carrots

¼ cucumber, halved lengthways, deseeded

10 g/¼ oz fresh mint, leaves torn from stems

10 g/¼ oz fresh coriander

55 g/2 oz beansprouts, rinsed and drained

½ cos lettuce heart, leaves shredded

6 x 20-cm/8-inch rice spring roll wrappers

Dipping sauce

juice of 1 lime

1 tbsp tamari

1 tbsp light muscovado sugar

1 tsp Thai fish sauce

1 red chilli, halved, deseeded and finely chopped

2 garlic cloves, finely chopped

2.5-cm/1-inch piece fresh ginger, scrubbed and finely grated

Method

1 Add the noodles to a shallow dish, cover with just-boiled water, then leave them to soften for 5 minutes.

2 Rinse the prawns in cold water and drain, then thickly slice and mix with the lime zest. Cut the carrots and cucumber into matchstick strips.

3 Arrange the mint, coriander, beansprouts, carrot sticks, cucumber sticks and shredded lettuce in separate piles on a tray.

4 Drain the noodles and tip into a dish. Pour some just-boiled water into a large, shallow round dish, then dip one of the rice wrappers into the water. Keep moving in the water for 10–15 seconds until soft and transparent, then lift out, draining well, and place on a chopping board.

5 Arrange a few prawns in a horizontal line in the centre of the rice wrapper, leaving a border of wrapper at either end. Top with some mint leaves and coriander sprigs, then add a few noodles and beansprouts.

6 Add some carrot and cucumber, and a little lettuce. Roll up the bottom third of the rice wrapper over the filling, fold in the sides, then roll up tightly to form a sausage shape. Set aside while you make the rest.

7 Repeat with the remaining wrappers until you have six rolls. To make the dip, add the lime juice to a small bowl, stir in the tamari, sugar and fish sauce, then add the chopped chilli, garlic and ginger, and stir.

8 Cut each roll in half and serve immediately with individual bowls of the dipping sauce. If planning to serve later, wrap each roll in clingfilm and chill in the refrigerator for up to 8 hours.

SWEET POTATO FRIES

Serves: 4   **Prep: 15 mins**   **Cook: 20 mins**

Ingredients

2 sprays of vegetable oil spray

900 g/2 lb sweet potatoes

½ tsp salt

½ tsp ground cumin

¼ tsp cayenne pepper

Method

1 Preheat the oven to 230°C/450°F/Gas Mark 8. Spray a large baking tray with vegetable oil spray.

2 Cut the sweet potatoes into 5-mm/¼-inch thick chips. Arrange them on the prepared baking tray in a single layer and spray them with vegetable oil spray.

3 Mix together the salt, cumin and cayenne pepper in a small bowl, then sprinkle the mixture evenly over the sweet potatoes and toss well.

4 Bake for 15–20 minutes, or until cooked through and lightly coloured. Serve hot.

BRAZILIAN GREENS WITH BLACK BEANS & ORANGES

Serves: 4   **Prep: 25 mins**   **Cook: 25 mins**

Ingredients

1 large orange

3 tbsp olive oil

1 small onion, finely chopped

1 garlic clove, finely chopped

1 fresh green chilli, deseeded and finely chopped

600 g/1 lb 5 oz kale, thick stalks removed and leaves sliced crossways

6–8 tbsp vegetable stock or chicken stock

400 g/14 oz canned black beans, drained and rinsed

6 tbsp chopped fresh coriander

1 tbsp olive oil, for drizzling

salt and pepper (optional)

Method

1 Using a sharp knife, cut a slice from the top and bottom of the orange. Remove the peel and white pith by cutting downwards, following the shape of the fruit as closely as possible. Working over a bowl, cut between the flesh and membrane of each segment and ease out the flesh. Slice each segment in half. Squeeze the membrane over the bowl to extract the juice.

2 Heat the oil in a large frying pan over a medium heat. Add the onion and fry for 5 minutes, until soft. Add the garlic and chilli, and fry for a further 2 minutes.

3 Gradually stir in the kale. Add a splash of stock, then cover and cook for 5–6 minutes, or until just wilted. Add more stock if the leaves start to look dry. Stir in the orange juice and any remaining stock. Season to taste with salt and pepper, if using, then cover and cook for 5 minutes, until the kale is tender.

4 Stir in the beans and the orange segments. Simmer, uncovered, for a few minutes to heat through. Stir in the coriander, drizzle with a little oil and serve immediately.

ROASTED ROOT VEGETABLES

Serves: 4–6   **Prep: 15 mins**   **Cook: 1 hr**

Ingredients

3 parsnips, cut into 5-cm/2-inch chunks

4 baby turnips, cut into quarters

3 carrots, cut into 5-cm/2-inch chunks

450 g/1 lb butternut squash, cut into 5-cm/2-inch chunks

450 g/1 lb sweet potatoes, cut into 5-cm/2-inch chunks

2 garlic cloves, finely chopped

2 tbsp chopped fresh rosemary

2 tbsp chopped fresh thyme

2 tsp chopped fresh sage

3 tbsp olive oil

salt and pepper (optional)

2 tbsp chopped fresh mixed herbs, such as parsley, thyme and mint, to garnish

Method

1 Preheat the oven to 220°C/425°F/Gas Mark 7.

2 Arrange all the vegetables in a single layer in a large roasting tin. Scatter over the garlic, rosemary, thyme and sage. Pour over the oil and season well with salt and pepper, if using.

3 Toss all the ingredients together until they are well mixed and coated with the oil (you can leave them to marinate at this stage to allow the flavours to be absorbed).

4 Roast the vegetables at the top of the preheated oven for 50–60 minutes, until they are cooked and nicely browned. Turn the vegetable over halfway through the cooking time. Serve immediately, garnished with the mixed herbs.

ROASTED BROCCOLI WITH PINE NUTS & PARMESAN

Serves: 4 | **Prep: 20 mins** | **Cook: 25 mins**

Ingredients

1 head of broccoli, weighing 800 g/1 lb 12 oz

6 tbsp olive oil

1 tsp sea salt

¼ tsp pepper

4 tbsp toasted pine nuts

grated zest of ½ lemon

25 g/1 oz Parmesan cheese shavings

4 lemon wedges, to garnish

Method

1 Preheat the oven to 230°C/450°F/Gas Mark 8. Cut off the broccoli crown where it meets the stalk. Remove the outer peel from the stalk. Slice the stalk crossways into 8-cm/3¼-inch pieces, then quarter each slice lengthways. Cut the crown into 4-cm/1½-inch wide wedges.

2 Put the broccoli wedges and stalks in a bowl. Sprinkle with the oil, salt and pepper, gently tossing to coat. Spread out in a large roasting tin. Cover tightly with foil and roast the broccoli on the bottom rack of the preheated oven for 10 minutes.

3 Remove the foil, then roast for a further 5–8 minutes, until just starting to brown. Turn the stalks and wedges over, and roast for a further 3–5 minutes, until tender.

4 Tip into a shallow, warmed serving dish, together with any cooking juices. Sprinkle with the pine nuts and lemon zest, tossing to mix. Scatter the cheese shavings over the top.

5 Garnish with lemon wedges and serve hot, warm or at room temperature.

STUFFED AUBERGINES

Serves: 4   **Prep: 30 mins**   **Cook: 50 mins**

Ingredients

2 aubergines

1 tbsp virgin olive oil

1 small onion,
finely chopped

2 garlic cloves,
finely chopped

140 g/5 oz white quinoa

350 ml/12 fl oz home-made
vegetable stock

25 g/1 oz unblanched
almonds, thinly sliced
and toasted

2 tbsp finely chopped
fresh mint, plus
a few sprigs to garnish

85 g/3 oz feta cheese,
drained and crumbled

salt and pepper (optional)

Method

1 Preheat the oven to 230°C/450°F/Gas Mark 8.
   Put the aubergines on a baking sheet and bake
   for 15 minutes, or until soft. Leave to cool slightly.

2 Cut each aubergine in half lengthways and
   scoop out the flesh, leaving a 5-mm/¼-inch-thick
   border inside the skin so they hold their shape.
   Chop the flesh.

3 Heat the oil in a large, heavy-based frying
   pan over a medium–high heat. Add the onion
   and garlic and cook, stirring occasionally, for
   5 minutes, or until soft. Add the quinoa, stock
   and aubergine flesh, and season with salt and
   pepper, if using. Reduce the heat to medium–
   low, cover and cook for 15 minutes, or until the
   quinoa is cooked through. Remove from the
   heat and stir in the sliced almonds, mint and
   half the feta.

4 Divide the quinoa mixture equally among the
   aubergine skins and top with the remaining
   feta. Bake for 10–15 minutes, or until the feta is
   bubbling and beginning to brown. Garnish with
   the mint sprigs and serve.

BUTTERNUT WEDGES WITH SAGE & PUMPKIN SEEDS

Serves: 3   **Prep: 20 mins**   **Cook: 35 mins**

Ingredients

1 large butternut squash

1 tbsp olive oil

½ tsp chilli powder

12 fresh sage leaves, finely chopped

50 g/1¾ oz pumpkin seeds

salt and pepper (optional)

Method

1 Preheat the oven to 200°C/400°F/Gas Mark 6. Prepare the butternut squash by washing any excess dirt from the skin and slicing off the very top and very bottom.

2 Using a sharp knife and a steady hand, cut the squash into six long wedges. Scoop out any seeds and discard. Place the wedges on a baking tray. Brush with half of the olive oil and sprinkle with the chilli powder. Roast in the preheated oven for 25 minutes.

3 Remove from the oven and brush with the remaining olive oil. Sprinkle over the sage and pumpkin seeds. Season with salt and pepper, if using, and return the wedges to the oven for a further 10 minutes. Serve immediately, garnished with extra pepper, if using.

SNACKS & SIDES

ROAST CAULIFLOWER WITH PARMESAN

Serves: 4   **Prep: 10 mins**   **Cook: 30 mins**

Ingredients

head of cauliflower, cut
into small florets

2 tbsp extra virgin
rapeseed oil

¼ tsp salt

½ tsp pepper

1 tsp Italian seasoning

1 tsp garlic purée

1 tbsp lemon juice

5 tbsp freshly grated
Parmesan cheese

Method

1 Preheat the oven to 200°C/400°F/Gas Mark 6.
   Line a baking tray with baking paper.

2 Place the cauliflower florets in a bowl and toss
   with the oil, salt, pepper, Italian seasoning, garlic
   and lemon juice.

3 Transfer the cauliflower mixture to the prepared
   tray and roast in the preheated oven for 20
   minutes, turning over halfway through the
   cooking time.

4 Sprinkle over the Parmesan cheese and roast
   for a further 10 minutes, or until the cheese and
   cauliflower are a light golden colour and the
   cauliflower is tender when pierced with a sharp
   knife. Serve immediately.

SNACKS & SIDES

SPICED CARROT MASH

Serves: 4

Prep: 20 mins, plus cooling

Cook: 30–35 mins

Ingredients

1.25 kg/2 lb 12 oz carrots, cut in half lengthways

1 small bulb of garlic cloves, peeled

1 tsp ground turmeric

1 tsp ground coriander

1 tsp ground cumin

2 tbsp olive oil

salt and pepper (optional)

2 tsp black onion seeds, to garnish

1 tbsp roughly chopped flat-leaf parsley, to garnish (optional)

Method

1 Preheat the oven to 200°C/400°F/Gas Mark 6.

2 Place the carrots, garlic cloves, turmeric, coriander and cumin in a large roasting tin. Drizzle over the olive oil and stir well, until the carrots are thoroughly coated. Season with salt and pepper, if using.

3 Roast in the preheated oven for 30–35 minutes, or until soft. Turn once, about halfway through, to ensure even cooking.

4 Remove from the oven and leave to cool slightly. Firmly mash the carrot mixture until you have a soft consistency, adding a touch of hot water if needed. Season again to taste, if desired.

5 Serve immediately in a warmed serving dish, garnished with black onion seeds and parsley, if desired.

RADICCHIO, ORANGE & POMEGRANATE SIDE SALAD

Serves: 4   **Prep: 10 mins**   **Cook: No cooking**

Ingredients

1 small head red radicchio

100 g/3½ oz curly endive leaves

2 oranges, cut into segments

seeds from 1 small pomegranate

2 tbsp olive oil

2 tsp pomegranate molasses

2 tsp white wine vinegar

½ tsp salt

1 tsp pepper

1 tsp lightly crushed cumin seeds

3 tbsp chopped fresh flat-leaf parsley, to garnish

Method

1 Roughly tear the radicchio leaves and arrange them on a serving platter with the curly endive leaves scattered around. Place the orange segments on top of the radicchio leaves and scatter over the pomegranate seeds.

2 Whisk together the oil, molasses, vinegar, salt, pepper and cumin seeds and drizzle over the salad. Garnish with the parsley and serve the salad immediately.

GRIDDLED AUBERGINE & BULGAR WHEAT SALAD

Serves: 2   **Prep: 15 mins**   **Cook: 10 mins**

Ingredients

70 g/2½ oz bulgar wheat

2 tbsp chopped fresh parsley

1 tbsp chopped fresh mint

1 large aubergine

1 large courgette, cut into 1-cm/½-inch slices

2 tbsp olive oil

1 tbsp lemon juice

½ tsp salt

½ tsp pepper

½ tsp smoked paprika

1½ tbsp toasted pine nuts

2 spring onions, chopped

Method

1 Put the bulgar wheat into a heatproof bowl and pour over 150 ml/5 fl oz of boiling water. Set aside for 15 minutes, then fluff up with a fork. Stir in the parsley and mint.

2 Meanwhile, cut the aubergine into 2-cm/¾-inch rounds, then halve each round. Brush the aubergine and courgette with the oil. Place a griddle pan over a high heat, then add the vegetables and cook for 8 minutes, turning halfway through, or until lightly charred and soft. Remove from the heat and sprinkle over the lemon juice, salt, pepper, paprika and any remaining oil.

3 Serve the vegetables on top of the bulgar wheat and garnish with the pine nuts and chopped spring onions.

CABBAGE, CARROT & ALMOND SIDE SALAD

Serves: 4

Prep: 15 mins,
plus standing

Cook: No cooking

Ingredients

100 g/3½ oz red cabbage, thinly sliced

100 g/3½ oz white cabbage, thinly sliced

1 large carrot, grated

1 small red onion, thinly sliced

25 g/1 oz flaked almonds, toasted

5 ready-to-eat dried apricots, chopped

2 tbsp extra virgin rapeseed oil

juice of ½ lemon

1 tsp Dijon mustard

½ tsp salt

1 tsp pepper

2 tsp maple syrup

4 tbsp fresh coriander leaves

1 tbsp fresh coriander leaves, to garnish

Method

1 Put the red cabbage, white cabbage, carrot, onion, almonds and apricots into a large bowl and stir to combine.

2 Mix the oil, lemon juice, mustard, salt, pepper and maple syrup together in a small bowl, then whisk until combined. Stir into the salad until everything is thoroughly coated. Cover and leave to stand at room temperature for a few hours for the flavours to blend.

3 Before serving, stir in the fresh coriander. Garnish with a few leaves on top and serve immediately.

★ Variation

Replace the sauce with a lime and miso dressing. Place one tablespoon each of fish sauce, rice vinegar and miso paste in a jar. Add the zest and juice of two limes and two tablespoons of sesame oil. Season with salt and pepper and shake.

LUNCH

TURKEY SOUP WITH MULTIGRAINS

Serves: 4

Prep: 20–25 mins, plus soaking

Cook: 40 mins

Ingredients

85 g/3 oz aduki beans, soaked overnight in cold water

85 g/3 oz oat groats

55 g/2 oz freekeh

1 tbsp olive oil

150 g/5½ oz leeks, green and white parts separated and thinly sliced

250 g/9 oz turkey breast meat, diced

1.2 litres/2 pints chicken stock

20 g/¾ oz fresh ginger, peeled and chopped

150 g/5½ oz frozen soya beans

85 g/3 oz baby spinach leaves

juice of 1 lemon

salt and pepper (optional)

Method

1 Half fill a medium-sized saucepan with water, bring to the boil, then add the drained beans, the oat groats and the freekeh. Bring back to the boil and boil briskly for 10 minutes.

2 Meanwhile, heat the oil in a second saucepan, add the white leek slices and the turkey breast and fry over a medium heat, stirring, for 5 minutes until just beginning to colour.

3 Pour the stock into the turkey pan, then add the ginger. Drain the partly cooked grains, add to the pan, then bring to the boil, stirring. Cover and simmer for 25 minutes.

4 Add the soya beans, spinach and green leek slices. Cover and simmer for 5 minutes. Stir in the lemon juice, then add salt and pepper to taste, using. Ladle into shallow bowls and serve.

★ **Variation**

Serve the soup with croûtons sprinkled over the top. Preheat the oven to 150°C/300°F/Gas Mark 2. Cut two slices of wholemeal bread into cubes. Toss the bread with two tablespoons of olive oil and arrange the cubes on a baking sheet in a single layer, then bake for 25 minutes.

PROTEIN RICE BOWL

Serves: 2 **Prep: 25 mins** **Cook: 30 mins**

Ingredients

150 g/5½ oz brown rice

2 large eggs

70 g/2½ oz spinach

4 spring onions, finely chopped

1 red chilli, deseeded and finely sliced

½ ripe avocado, sliced

2 tbsp roasted peanuts

Vinaigrette

2 tbsp olive oil

1 tsp Dijon mustard

1 tbsp cider vinegar

juice of ½ lemon

Method

1 Place the rice in a large saucepan and cover with twice the volume of water. Bring to the boil and simmer for 25 minutes, or until the rice is tender and the liquid has nearly all disappeared. Continue to simmer for a further few minutes if some liquid remains.

2 Meanwhile, cook your eggs. Bring a small saucepan of water to the boil. Carefully add the eggs to the pan and boil for 7 minutes – the whites will be cooked and the yolks should still be very slightly soft. Drain and pour cold water over the eggs to stop them cooking. When cool enough to handle, tap them on the work surface to crack the shells and peel them. Cut the eggs into quarters.

3 Stir the spinach, half of the spring onions and a little red chilli into the cooked rice.

4 To make the vinaigrette, whisk the olive oil, Dijon mustard, cider vinegar and lemon juice together. Pour the dressing over the warm rice and mix thoroughly to combine.

5 Divide the rice between two bowls and top each with the remaining spring onions, avocado, remaining red chilli, peanuts and egg quarters.

TOFU & EDAMAME NOODLE BROTH BOWL

Serves: 4

Prep: 15 mins, plus marinating

Cook: 15 mins

Ingredients

2 tbsp low-salt soy sauce

2 tbsp rice vinegar

1 tbsp mirin

250 g/9 oz firm silken tofu, cut into 12 pieces

15 g/½ oz cornflour

1 tbsp groundnut oil

1 litre/1¾ pints reduced-salt vegetable stock

250 g/9 oz buckwheat soba noodles

125 g/4½ oz frozen edamame beans

85 g/3 oz tenderstem broccoli stems

1 tbsp miso paste

½ tbsp sesame oil

6 spring onions, sliced

2.5 -cm/1-inch piece fresh ginger, peeled and finely chopped

1 red chilli, deseeded and thinly sliced

4 tbsp fresh coriander leaves, to garnish

Method

1 Combine the soy sauce, vinegar and mirin in a small bowl. Place the tofu in a shallow non-metallic bowl in a single layer and spoon over the soy marinade. Leave to marinate for at least 30 minutes, turning once.

2 Scatter the cornflour on a plate. Remove the tofu from the marinade, reserving the marinade, and coat in the cornflour. Heat the groundnut oil in a large frying pan over a medium–high heat. Add the tofu to the pan and fry, turning once or twice, until golden and crisp all over. Remove with a slotted spatula, drain on kitchen paper, set aside and keep warm.

3 Put the stock into a saucepan with the reserved marinade, noodles, edamame beans and broccoli and bring to a simmer. Cook for 5 minutes, or until the noodles and vegetables are just tender. Stir in the miso paste.

4 Meanwhile, add the sesame oil to the frying pan and place over a high heat. Stir-fry the spring onions, ginger and chilli for 1 minute.

5 To serve, divide the noodle soup among four bowls, top with the tofu pieces and then the spring onion mixture. Garnish with the coriander leaves and serve immediately.

SEVEN SEAS SOUP

Serves: 4   **Prep: 20–25 mins**   **Cook: 50 mins**

Ingredients

1 tbsp olive oil

1 onion, finely chopped

2 garlic cloves, finely chopped

1 small fennel bulb, green fronds reserved, bulb finely chopped

1 red pepper, halved, deseeded and diced

500 g/1 lb 2 oz tomatoes, peeled and diced

1.2 litres/2 pints vegetable stock

55 g/2 oz short-grain brown rice

½ tsp dried oregano

¼ tsp crushed dried red chillies

1 tbsp tomato purée

40 g/1½ oz canned dressed brown crabmeat

150 g/5½ oz prepared squid, sliced, thawed if frozen

225 g/8 oz raw prawns, peeled and deveined and thawed if frozen

225 g/8 oz cooked, shelled mussels, thawed if frozen

2 tbsp chopped fresh parsley

grated zest of 1 lemon

salt and pepper (optional)

Method

1 Heat the oil in a large saucepan, add the onion and fry over a medium heat, stirring, for 5 minutes until soft and just beginning to colour. Stir in the garlic, fennel, red pepper and tomatoes and cook for 3 minutes.

2 Pour in the stock, then add the rice, oregano, chillies and tomato purée. Bring to the boil, stirring, then cover and simmer for 30 minutes until the rice is tender.

3 Stir the crabmeat into the soup, then add the squid, prawns and mussels and cook for 5 minutes until all the prawns are bright pink. Add salt and pepper to taste, if using.

4 Chop the reserved fennel fronds and mix with the parsley and lemon zest. Ladle the soup into warmed shallow bowls, sprinkle the herb mix on top and serve immediately.

LUNCH

CHORIZO & KALE SOUP

Serves: 6   **Prep: 15–20 mins**   **Cook: 35 mins**

Ingredients

3 tbsp olive oil

1 Spanish onion, finely chopped

2 garlic cloves, finely chopped

900 g/2 lb potatoes, diced

1.5 litres/2½ pints vegetable stock

125 g/4½ oz chorizo or other spicy sausage, thinly sliced

450 g/1 lb kale or Savoy cabbage, cored and shredded

salt and pepper (optional)

Method

1. Heat 2 tablespoons of the oil in a large saucepan. Add the onion and garlic and cook over a low heat, stirring occasionally, for 5 minutes, until softened. Add the potatoes and cook, stirring constantly, for a further 3 minutes.

2. Increase the heat to medium, pour in the stock and bring to the boil. Reduce the heat, cover and cook for 10 minutes.

3. Meanwhile, heat the remaining oil in a frying pan. Add the chorizo and cook over a low heat, turning occasionally, for a few minutes, until the fat runs. Remove with a slotted spoon and drain on kitchen paper.

4. Remove the pan of soup from the heat and crush the potatoes with a potato masher. Return to the heat, add the kale and bring back to the boil. Reduce the heat and simmer for 5–6 minutes, until tender.

5. Remove the pan from the heat and crush the potatoes again. Stir in the chorizo and season to taste with salt and pepper, if using. Ladle into warmed bowls and serve immediately.

LUNCH

SWEET RED PEPPER & TOMATO SOUP

Serves: 4   **Prep: 10 mins**   **Cook: 35 mins**

Ingredients

1 tbsp olive oil

2 tbsp cold water

2 red peppers, deseeded and finely chopped

1 garlic clove, finely chopped

1 onion, finely chopped

400 g/14 oz canned chopped tomatoes

1.2 litres/2 pints vegetable stock

salt and pepper (optional)

fresh basil leaves, to garnish

Method

1 Put the oil, water, peppers, garlic and onion in a saucepan over a medium–low heat and cook for 5–10 minutes, or until all the vegetables have softened. Cover and simmer for 10 minutes.

2 Add the tomatoes and stock and season with salt and pepper, if using. Simmer, uncovered, for 15 minutes. Serve garnished with basil leaves.

LUNCH

KEEN GREEN SOUP

Serves: 2 **Prep: 10–15 mins** **Cook: No cooking**

Ingredients

180 g/6¼ oz cucumber

2 celery sticks

2 tbsp chopped
fresh parsley, plus
2 extra sprigs, to garnish

tbsp chopped fresh mint

2 tbsp chopped
fresh coriander

50 ml/9 fl oz chilled water

Method

1 Chop the cucumber and celery and add to a blender with the parsley, mint, coriander and water. Blend until smooth.

2 Serve immediately or chill in the refrigerator and stir just before serving, garnished with parsley.

LUNCH

BUTTERNUT SQUASH & MIXED SEED SALAD

Serves: 4　　　　**Prep: 20 mins**　　　　**Cook: 30 mins**

Ingredients

800 g/1 lb 12oz butternut squash, cut into 4-cm/1½-inch x 2-cm/¾-inch pieces

3 tbsp extra virgin rapeseed oil

1 large yellow pepper

125 g/4½ oz broccoli florets

juice of 1 small lemon

2 tsp maple syrup

1 tsp Dijon mustard

½ tsp salt

1 tsp pepper

150 g/5½ oz skimmed milk ricotta cheese

1½ tbsp pumpkin seeds

1 tbsp sunflower seeds

2 tsp poppy seeds

Method

1 Preheat the oven to 190°C/375°F/Gas Mark 5. Brush the squash pieces with some of the oil, then place on a large baking tray with the yellow pepper (leave it whole and do not brush with oil). Roast the vegetables in the preheated oven for approximately 30 minutes, turning halfway through. Check that the squash pieces are tender and the pepper has some charred patches and is soft – you may need to remove the pepper from the oven earlier than the squash.

2 When the pepper is cooked, put it in a polythene bag and seal. Leave for 10 minutes, by which time the charred skin should be easy to peel off. After peeling, halve and deseed the pepper and cut into slices.

3 Meanwhile, steam the broccoli florets until just tender and drain. Combine the remaining oil with the lemon juice, maple syrup, mustard, salt and pepper to make a dressing.

4 Arrange the squash on a serving platter with the broccoli florets and yellow pepper. Dot the vegatables with spoonfuls of the ricotta cheese, then scatter over the seeds. Give the dressing a really good stir and spoon it all over the salad. Serve immediately.

TURKEY FARRO SALAD

Serves: 2 **Prep: 10 mins** **Cook: 15 mins**

Ingredients

100 g/3½ oz quick-cook farro

500 ml/17 fl oz water

1½ tbsp walnut oil

½ tbsp lemon juice

1 tsp French mustard

1 tsp maple syrup

½ tsp garlic purée

1½ tbsp fresh coriander leaves

1½ tbsp chopped fresh flat-leaf parsley

1 small orange, sliced

1 small mango, sliced

1 small head chicory leaves, separated

175 g/6 oz cooked turkey breast, sliced

15 g/½ oz walnuts, chopped

salt (optional)

Method

1 Place the farro in a saucepan with the water and a little salt, if using. Bring to a simmer and cook for 10–12 minutes, or until the grains are cooked but still with a slightly chewy texture. Drain in a sieve.

2 Meanwhile, beat together the oil, lemon juice, mustard, maple syrup and garlic in a small bowl.

3 Stir two thirds of the oil mixture into the farro, while the grains are still slightly warm. Stir in two thirds of the coriander and parsley.

4 Arrange the farro salad on a serving platter with the fruit slices, chicory leaves and turkey slices on top. Drizzle over the remaining oil mixture, then sprinkle over the walnuts and remaining herbs. Serve immediately.

LUNCH

TUNA &
ASPARAGUS SALAD

Serves: 4　　　　　**Prep: 10 mins**　　　　　**Cook: 25 mins**

Ingredients

175 g/6 oz quinoa, rinsed

8 quail eggs

6 sprays cooking oil spray

24 asparagus spears, woody stems discarded

4 tuna steaks, each weighing 100 g/3½ oz

2 tbsp olive oil

½ tbsp white wine vinegar

½ tsp Dijon mustard

½ tsp sugar

½ tsp salt

½ tsp pepper

12 cherry tomatoes, halved

4 small spring onions, finely chopped, to garnish

Method

1 Bring a saucepan of water to the boil and add the quinoa. Cook for 15–18 minutes, or until just tender. Drain and set aside.

2 Meanwhile, bring a separate saucepan of water to the boil and add the eggs. Cook for 3 minutes, then drain and rinse in cold water to cool. Peel and halve the eggs.

3 Place a ridged griddle pan over a high heat and spray with 2 sprays of cooking spray. Add the asparagus spears and cook, turning once, for 4 minutes, or until they are slightly charred and just tender.

4 Spray the tuna steaks with the remaining cooking oil spray and cook in the griddle pan for 1½ minutes. Turn and cook for a further minute, or until cooked to your liking. Transfer to a plate and leave to rest for 2 minutes.

5 Beat together the olive oil, vinegar, mustard, sugar, salt and pepper in a small bowl. Stir two thirds of this oil mixture into the cooked quinoa.

6 Cut each tuna steak into three pieces. Divide the quinoa among four serving plates and top evenly with the tuna pieces, asparagus, eggs and tomatoes. Drizzle the remaining dressing over the top and garnish with the spring onions.

HOT-SMOKED SALMON WITH CUCUMBER SALAD

Serves: 2

Prep: 10 mins,
plus standing

Cook: No cooking

Ingredients

250 g/9 oz hot-smoked salmon

1 tbsp creamed horseradish

3 tbsp Greek-style yogurt

½ tsp pepper

30 g/1 oz fresh pea shoots, to garnish

2 slices dark rye bread, each weighing 30 g/1 oz, to serve

Cucumber salad

10 -cm/4 -inch piece cucumber, peeled and cut into thin strips

1 tsp caster sugar

1 tbsp chopped fresh dill

1 tbsp white wine vinegar

Method

1 To make the salad, put the cucumber into a shallow non-metallic bowl. Stir the sugar and dill into the vinegar, then spoon this mixture evenly over the cucumber. Set aside for 30 minutes.

2 Meanwhile, bring the salmon to room temperature if it has been in the refrigerator. Cut into eight pieces and arrange four pieces on each serving plate.

3 Beat the horseradish with the yogurt in a small bowl. Stir in the pepper and spoon the mixture over the salmon. Divide the cucumber salad between the plates, spooning over any dressing remaining in the cucumber dish.

4 Garnish with the pea shoots and serve with the sliced rye bread.

SALAD-PACKED OPEN SANDWICH

Serves: 1   **Prep: 10 mins**   **Cook: 2 mins**

Ingredients

15 g/½ oz pine nuts

100 g/3½ oz low-fat cream cheese

1 thick slice of mixed grain bread, weighing 70 g/2½ oz

1 tomato, sliced

3 -cm/1¼ -inch piece cucumber, sliced

½ small avocado, sliced

10 g/¼ oz wild rocket

2 fresh basil sprigs, leaves picked and torn

1 tbsp aged balsamic vinegar

½ tsp pepper

2 tsp freshly grated Parmesan cheese

Method

1 Place a small frying pan over a high heat, add the pine nuts and toast until golden. Spread the cream cheese on the bread.

2 Arrange the tomato, cucumber and avocado slices on top of the bread. Sprinkle over the rocket and basil.

3 Sprinkle over the pine nuts, vinegar and pepper and finish with the cheese. Cut into quarters and serve immediately.

RED PEPPER HUMMUS, ROCKET & ARTICHOKE WRAPS

erves: 4

Prep: 10 mins, plus cooling

Cook: 5–10 mins

Ingredients

1 large red pepper, seeded and quartered

400 g/14 oz canned chickpeas, drained and rinsed

2 tbsp lemon juice

2 tbsp tahini

and pepper (optional)

4 wholemeal tortillas

) g/1½ oz rocket leaves

g/7 oz artichoke hearts in oil, drained and quartered

Method

1 Preheat a grill to high. Place the pepper quarters, cut-side down, on a grill pan and grill until the skins are blackened and charred. Put the peppers in a polythene bag, seal and leave to cool.

2 To make the hummus, remove the skins from the peppers and place in a food processor with the chickpeas, lemon juice and tahini. Process until almost smooth. Season to taste with salt and pepper, if using.

3 Divide the hummus among the tortillas, placing the hummus down the centre of each wrap. Top with the rocket leaves and artichoke hearts.

4 Fold the tortilla sides over to enclose the filling and serve immediately.

LUNCH

TURKEY, MOZZARELLA & PEPPER PANINI

Serves: 4

Prep: 10 mins, plus cooling

Cook: 10 mins

Ingredients

2 red peppers, halved and deseeded

4 ciabatta rolls

200 g/7 oz roast turkey breast, sliced

125 g/4½ oz half-fat mozzarella, sliced

handful of basil leaves

2 tbsp sweet chilli sauce

Method

1 Preheat a grill to hot. Place the peppers cut-side down on a grill pan and cook under the preheated grill for 4–6 minutes, or until the skins are blackened and charred. Put the peppers in a polythene bag, seal and leave to cool. Remove the skins once cool.

2 Split the rolls open and arrange the turkey on the bottom halves. Top with the mozzarella and basil leaves. Drizzle with chilli sauce.

3 Slice the peppers thickly, then arrange over the other ingredients in the rolls.

4 Place a griddle pan over a high heat and cook the panini, pressing down lightly with a fish slice or place under a hot grill, until golden brown. Serve immediately.

LUNCH

GRIDDLED MACKEREL ON RYE BREAD

Serves: 4　　**Prep: 10 mins**　　**Cook: 10 mins**

Ingredients

4 mackerel fillets, each
weighing 125 g/4½ oz

4 slices dark rye bread,
each weighing 50 g/1¾ oz

4 tbsp chopped fresh flat-
leaf parsley, to garnish

Anchovy relish

4 tbsp chopped fresh
flat-leaf parsley

2 tbsp capers from a jar,
drained

2 tsp Dijon mustard

6 anchovy fillets in oil,
drained

juice of ½ lemon

1 tsp pepper

2 tbsp extra virgin olive oil

Method

1 To make the relish, place the parsley, capers, mustard, anchovy fillets and lemon juice in a blender or food processor and whizz for a few seconds to blend. Alternatively, very finely chop the parsley, capers and anchovies and stir them together with the mustard and lemon juice in a small bowl. Stir the pepper and oil into the relish and set aside.

2 Place a ridged griddle pan over a high heat, then add the mackerel fillets and cook for 2–3 minutes on each side until cooked through. Meanwhile, toast the rye bread.

3 Place the mackerel on the toasted bread and drizzle over the relish. Garnish with the parsley and serve immediately.

LUNCH

GRIDDLED TURKEY WHOLEGRAIN WRAPS

Serves: 2 | **Prep: 10 mins** | **Cook: 5 mins**

Ingredients

225 g/8 oz fresh turkey breast mince

pinch of paprika

pinch of dried oregano

½ tsp pepper

1 egg white

2 tbsp low-fat cream cheese

2 tbsp extra-light mayonnaise

1 tbsp medium-hot peri peri sauce

6 sprays light cooking oil spray

2 tomatoes, each cut into 4 slices

2 wholegrain wraps, each 20 cm/8 inches in diameter

6 crisp Little Gem lettuce leaves, torn

30 g/1 oz mild salsa dip

Method

1 Combine the turkey mince, paprika, oregano, pepper and egg white in a large bowl. Shape the mixture into 10 small patties.

2 In a small bowl, beat together the cream cheese, mayonnaise and peri peri sauce.

3 Place a ridged griddle pan over a medium heat. Spray the turkey patties and the tomato slices with the cooking oil spray. Add the turkey patties to the pan. Cook for 2 minutes on one side until golden, then turn the patties over. Add the tomato slices to the pan and cook for a further 2 minutes, or until the patties are cooked through and the tomatoes are soft. Check that the patties are no longer pink in the centre and are piping hot.

4 Spread the wraps with the cream cheese mixture and top evenly with the lettuce, patties and tomatoes. Spoon the mild salsa dip evenly over each wrap. Fold up the wraps and serve immediately.

KALE & GREEN GARLIC BRUSCHETTA

Serves: 4 **Prep: 25 mins** **Cook: 25 mins**

Ingredients

1 green garlic bulb

3 tbsp olive oil

4 slices sourdough bread with mixed or sprouted seeds, total weight 250 g/9 oz

85 g/3 oz shredded kale, rinsed well and drained

1 tbsp balsamic vinegar

2 tsp pomegranate molasses

salt and pepper (optional)

Method

1 Preheat the oven to 190°C/375°F/Gas Mark 5. Put the garlic bulb on a piece of foil, drizzle with 1 tablespoon of the oil, then wrap the foil around it and seal well. Put on a baking sheet and roast in the preheated oven for 20 minutes, or until the bulb feels soft when squeezed.

2 Meanwhile, preheat a ridged griddle pan. Cut the bread slices in half, brush one side of each with a little oil, then cook the bread, oiled-side down, in the hot pan for 2 minutes. Brush the top with the remaining oil, then turn and cook the second side until golden brown.

3 Unwrap the garlic, peel away the outer casing from the bulb, separate the cloves, then remove any of the tougher skins. Crush the creamy soft garlic to a coarse paste using a pestle and mortar. Mix the paste with any juices from the foil, then thinly spread on the griddled bread and keep warm.

4 Heat a dry, non-stick frying pan, add the kale and cook over a medium heat for 2–3 minutes until just wilted. Mix in the vinegar, molasses and a little salt and pepper, if using. Arrange the bruschetta on a chopping board, spoon over the kale and serve.

MOROCCAN MEATBALLS

Serves: 4   **Prep: 35 mins**   **Cook: 15 mins**

Ingredients

olive oil spray

450 g/1 lb fresh lamb mince

½ small onion, finely chopped

1 garlic clove, finely chopped

1½ tsp ground cumin

1½ tsp salt

½ tsp pepper

¼ tsp ground cinnamon

1 egg

10 g/¼ oz fresh breadcrumbs

4 pittas

1 cucumber, diced

2 tbsp chopped fresh flat-leaf parsley

140 g/5 oz cherry tomatoes, halved

juice of 1 lemon

lemon wedges, to serve

Yogurt mint sauce

10 g/¼ oz fresh mint leaves

280 g/10 oz natural yogurt

juice of ½ lemon

½ tsp salt

¼ tsp cayenne pepper

Method

1 Preheat the oven to 190°C/375°F/Gas Mark 5 and spray a large baking sheet with oil. Put the lamb, onion, garlic, cumin, 1 teaspoon of salt, pepper, cinnamon, egg and breadcrumbs into a large bowl, mix well to combine and shape into 2.5-cm/1-inch balls.

2 Place the meatballs on the prepared baking sheet and spray with oil. Bake in the preheated oven for about 15 minutes, until cooked through

3 Meanwhile, wrap the pittas in foil and put them in the oven. To make the sauce, finely chop the mint. Put the mint into a small bowl with the remaining ingredients and stir well.

4 To make the salad, put the cucumber, parsley and tomatoes into a medium-sized bowl and mix to combine. Add the lemon juice and ½ teaspoon of salt and stir to combine.

5 Remove the meatballs and bread from the oven Cut the pittas in half. Stuff a few meatballs into each half and spoon in some of the sauce. Serve two halves per person with the salad and lemon wedges alongside.

LUNCH

QUINOA & BEETROOT BURGERS

Makes: 8　　　　**Prep: 35 mins**　　　　**Cook: 1hr 10 mins**

Ingredients

3-4 small beetroots, peeled and cubed, about 225 g/8 oz in total

135 g/4¾ oz quinoa, rinsed

350 ml/12 fl oz vegetable stock

½ small onion, grated

finely grated zest of ½ lemon

2 tsp cumin seeds

½ tsp salt

¼ tsp pepper

1 large egg white, lightly beaten

10 g/¼ oz quinoa flour, for dusting

1 tbsp vegetable oil, for shallow-frying

8 slices of sourdough toast, to serve

150 g/5½ oz peppery green salad leaves, to serve

Wasabi butter

1½ tsp wasabi powder

¾ tsp warm water

70 g/2½ oz butter, at room temperature

Method

1 Cook the beetroots in a steamer for 1 hour.

2 Meanwhile, put the quinoa into a saucepan with the stock. Bring to the boil, then cover and simmer over a very low heat for 10 minutes. Remove from the heat, but leave the pan covered for a further 10 minutes to allow the grains to swell. Fluff up with a fork and spread out on a tray to dry.

3 To make the wasabi butter, mix together the wasabi powder and water. Mix with the butter and chill in the refrigerator.

4 Place the beetroots in a food processor and process until smooth. Tip into a bowl and mix with the quinoa, onion, lemon zest, cumin seeds, salt, pepper and egg white.

5 Divide the mixture into eight equal-sized portions and shape into burgers, each 15 mm/⅝ inch thick, firmly pressing the mixture together. Lightly dust with quinoa flour.

6 Heat a thin layer of oil in a non-stick frying pan. Add the burgers and fry over a medium–high heat, in batches if necessary, for 2 minutes on each side, turning carefully.

7 Place the burgers on the toast and serve with the wasabi butter and salad leaves.

SPICY RICE WITH CHICKEN & POMEGRANATE

Serves: 4

Prep: 25 mins, plus cooling

Cook: 45–50 mins

Ingredients

4 large chicken thighs

2 tsp Chinese five spice

2 tbsp olive oil

2 red onions, finely sliced

2 garlic cloves, finely sliced

5 cardamom pods, crushed

2 star anise

250 g/9 oz brown rice

750 ml/1¼ pints vegetable stock

25 g/1 oz fresh mint, roughly chopped

25 g/1 oz fresh flat-leaf parsley, roughly chopped

seeds of 1 small pomegranate

4 tbsp toasted almonds

finely grated zest and juice of 1 lemon

salt and pepper (optional)

Method

1 Preheat the oven to 200°C/400°F/Gas Mark 6. Place the chicken thighs on a baking tray and sprinkle over the Chinese five spice. Drizzle over 1 tablespoon of olive oil and roast in the preheated oven for 20 minutes, or until the juices run clear when the thickest part of the meat is pierced and no traces of pink remain in the centre. Remove from the oven and let cool.

2 Meanwhile, heat the remaining olive oil in a saucepan over a medium–low heat. Add the onion and gently fry for 10–12 minutes, or until soft and starting to caramelize. Stir in the garlic, cardamom pods and star anise and cook for a further minute. Add the rice and stir well.

3 Pour in the stock and bring the pan to the boil. Cover and simmer gently for 25–30 minutes, or until all the stock has been absorbed and the rice is tender.

4 Once the chicken is cool enough to handle, remove the meat from the bones and finely slice. Add to the rice mixture, with any remaining juices, and season with salt and pepper, if using.

5 Stir in half of the mint and parsley. Top with the remaining herbs, pomegranate seeds, toasted almonds, lemon juice and zest and serve.

LUNCH

TURKEY GOUJONS WITH RED CABBAGE & KALE SLAW

Serves: 4   **Prep: 20 mins**   **Cook: 15 mins**

Ingredients

70 g/2½ oz linseeds

40 g/1½ oz sesame seeds

2 eggs

450 g/1 lb skinless and boneless turkey breast, thinly sliced

3 tbsp virgin olive oil

salt and pepper (optional)

Red cabbage and kale slaw

115 g/4 oz red cabbage, thinly shredded

25 g/1 oz kale, thinly shredded

1 carrot, coarsely grated

1 dessert apple, cored and roughly grated

1 tsp caraway seeds

60 g/2¼ oz Greek-style natural yogurt

Method

1 Preheat the oven to 220°C/425°F/Gas Mark 7 and put a large baking sheet in it.

2 To make the slaw, put the red cabbage, kale and carrot in a bowl and mix well. Add the apple, caraway seeds and yogurt, season with salt and pepper, if using, and mix well. Cover and chill in the refrigerator until needed.

3 Put the linseeds in a spice mill or blender and process until roughly chopped. Add the sesame seeds and process for a few seconds. Tip the mixture out onto a plate. Crack the eggs into a dish, season with salt and pepper, if using, and beat lightly with a fork.

4 Dip each turkey slice into the eggs, then lift it out with a fork and dip both sides into the seed mixture to coat. Brush the hot baking sheet with a little oil, add the turkey slices in a single layer, then drizzle with a little extra oil.

5 Bake the turkey, turning the slices once and moving them from the corners into the centre of the baking sheet, for 15 minutes, or until golden brown and cooked through. Cut one of the larger turkey goujons in half to check that the meat is no longer pink. Any juices that run out should be clear and piping hot with steam rising. Serve the goujons with the slaw.

HAM &
SWEET POTATO HASH

Serves: 4   **Prep: 15 mins**   **Cook: 35 mins**

Ingredients

250 g/9 oz floury potatoes, cut into 2-cm/¾-inch cubes, such as Maris Piper

2 tbsp water

2 tbsp extra virgin rapeseed oil

1 small red onion, very finely chopped

1 garlic clove, finely chopped

500 g/1 lb sweet potatoes, cut into 1.5 cm/½-inch cubes

200 g/7 oz lean cooked ham, diced

100 g/3½ oz canned chickpeas, drained and rinsed

1 tsp ground cumin seeds

1 tsp pepper

1 tsp dried chilli flakes (optional)

salt (optional)

Method

1 Place the floury potato cubes and the water in a microwaveable bowl and microwave on High for 4 minutes, or until partly cooked. Drain and dry the potato cubes on kitchen paper.

2 Place a large non-stick frying pan over a medium heat and add the oil. Add the onion and fry, stirring occasionally, for 5 minutes, or until soft and just beginning to brown. Add the garlic and stir for 30 seconds.

3 Add the floury and sweet potato cubes to the pan and cook, stirring gently occasionally, for 10 minutes. Stir in the ham and cook for a further 5 minutes. Check that the vegetables are tender when pierced with a sharp knife and nicely golden on the outside and that the ham has a little colour too.

4 Stir in the chickpeas, cumin, pepper, chilli flakes, if using, and salt, if using. Cook for a further 3–5 minutes, or until everything is warmed through, then serve immediately.

LOADED SWEET POTATOES

Serves: 4 **Prep: 20–25 mins** **Cook: 50–55 mins**

Ingredients

4 small sweet potatoes, scrubbed

1 tbsp olive oil

1 small onion, chopped

1 garlic clove, finely chopped

1 tsp ground coriander

½ tsp ground cumin

200 g/7 oz tomatoes, peeled and diced

2 tsp tomato purée

200 g/7 oz canned chickpeas, drained and rinsed

4 tbsp chopped fresh coriander

115 g/4 oz fat-free Greek-style yogurt

salt and pepper (optional)

Method

1 Preheat the oven to 190°C/375°F/Gas Mark 5. Prick the potatoes with a fork, put them on a baking sheet and bake in the preheated oven for 45–50 minutes, or until the potatoes feel soft when squeezed.

2 Meanwhile, heat the oil in a small frying pan, add the onion and fry over a medium heat for 4–5 minutes, until soft. Stir in the garlic, ground coriander and cumin, and cook the mixture for a further minute.

3 Mix in the tomatoes, tomato purée and chickpeas, then season with a little salt and pepper, if using. Cover and cook for 10 minutes, then remove from the heat and set aside.

4 Transfer the potatoes to a serving plate, slit each along its length and open out slightly. Reheat the chickpeas and spoon them over the potatoes. Mix half the fresh coriander into the yogurt and spoon over the chickpeas. Sprinkle with the remaining fresh coriander and serve the potatoes immediately.

LUNCH

LENTIL & GOAT'S CHEESE TOMATOES

Serves: 4　　　　**Prep: 15 mins**　　　　**Cook: 35–45 mins**

Ingredients

5 g/2 oz dried Puy lentils

4 beef tomatoes

1 tbsp olive oil

2 large shallots, finely chopped

1 garlic clove, crushed

1 tbsp chopped fresh thyme

100 g/3½ oz hard goat's cheese, diced

salt and pepper (optional)

Method

1　Bring a small saucepan of water to the boil over a medium–high heat. Add the lentils, return to the boil and cook for 20–25 minutes, or until tender. Drain well.

2　Meanwhile, preheat the oven to 200°C/400°F/ Gas Mark 6. Cut a slice from the tops of the tomatoes and set aside. Scoop out the pulp from the centre and chop roughly.

3　Heat the oil in a frying pan over a medium heat and fry the shallots, stirring, for 3–4 minutes to soften. Add the garlic and chopped tomato pulp and cook for a further 3–4 minutes, or until any excess moisture has evaporated.

4　Place the tomatoes in a shallow baking dish. Stir the lentils and thyme into the frying pan, and season to taste with salt and pepper, if using. Stir in the goat's cheese and then spoon the mixture into the tomatoes.

5　Replace the lids on the tomatoes and bake in the preheated oven for 15–20 minutes, or until tender. Serve immediately.

LUNCH

CRAYFISH CAKES WITH AVOCADO & CHILLI MASH

Serves: 2　　　　**Prep: 15 mins**　　　　**Cook: 10 mins**

Ingredients

30 g/1 oz wholemeal breadcrumbs

½ tsp pepper

2 tbsp finely chopped fresh flat-leaf parsley

200 g/7 oz peeled and cooked crayfish tails, roughly chopped

50 g/1¾ oz ready-roasted red pepper from a jar, drained and chopped

1 tsp medium-hot peri peri sauce

1 tbsp extra-light mayonnaise

1 small egg white, beaten

10 g/¼ oz flour, for dusting

6 sprays cooking oil spray

Avocado & chilli mash

1 ripe avocado, sliced

1 small fresh red chilli, deseeded and finely chopped

1 spring onion, finely chopped

½ tsp smoked paprika

juice of ¼ lime

Method

1 Put the breadcrumbs, pepper and parsley into a bowl and stir well to combine.

2 In a separate bowl, combine the crayfish tails, red pepper, peri peri sauce and mayonnaise. Stir the breadcrumb mixture into the crayfish mixture and mix well.

3 Add the beaten egg white and mix to a moderately firm mixture – the cakes will firm up more once they are cooked. Divide into four rough rounds and sprinkle with flour. If you have time, chill for up to 1 hour.

4 To make the mash, place the avocado slices in a bowl and roughly mash with a fork. Stir in the chilli, spring onion, paprika and lime juice.

5 Spray a non-stick frying pan with the cooking oil spray and place over a medium–high heat. Add the crayfish cakes and cook for 2–3 minutes, or until the underside is crisp and golden. Turn and cook for a further 2–3 minutes, or until cooked through. Serve the cakes immediately with the avocado mash on the side.

LUNCH

CHICKEN WITH RED CABBAGE & CHILLI COLESLAW

Serves: 4

Prep: 20 mins, plus marinating

Cook: 35 mins

Ingredients

200 ml/7 fl oz
soured cream

½ tsp cayenne pepper

1 garlic clove, crushed

4 chicken thighs
and 4 chicken drumsticks
(about 850 g/1 lb 14 oz)

2 tsp coarse polenta

2 tbsp quinoa flour

2 tbsp wholemeal
plain flour

vegetable oil,
for deep-frying

salt and pepper (optional)

Coleslaw

200 g/7 oz
red cabbage, shredded

400 g/14 oz
fennel, shredded

1 red chilli, deseeded and
thinly sliced lengthways

100 g/3½ oz Greek-style
natural yogurt

juice of ¼ lemon

Method

1 Put the soured cream, cayenne and garlic in a large bowl and season well with salt and pepper, if using. Add the chicken and toss well. Cover the bowl with clingfilm and chill in the refrigerator for 2–3 hours, or overnight if you have time.

2 To make the coleslaw, put all the ingredients in a large bowl and toss well, then season with salt and pepper, if using. Cover the coleslaw and chill in the refrigerator.

3 Mix together the polenta and flours on a plate and season with salt and pepper, if using. Half-fill a heavy-based frying pan with oil and place it over a medium–high heat. Heat the oil to 180°C/350°F, or until a cube of bread browns in 30 seconds. While it heats, sprinkle the flour mixture over the chicken.

4 Cook the chicken in two batches, as too much chicken in the pan will make the oil temperature drop. Using tongs, carefully place half the chicken in the oil. Cook for 6–8 minutes, then turn and cook for a further 6–8 minutes, until the coating is a deep golden brown, the chicken is cooked through to the bone, and the juices run clear with no sign of pink when a skewer is inserted into the thickest part of the meat.

LUNCH

Using a slotted spoon, transfer the cooked chicken to kitchen paper to drain, then keep warm in a low oven while you cook the second batch.

Serve the chicken on a sharing board with the coleslaw.

CHICKEN SATAY SKEWERS

Serves: 4

Prep: 25–30 mins, plus marinating

Cook: 6–8 mins

Ingredients

4 skinless, boneless chicken breasts, about 115 g/4 oz each, cut into 2-cm/¾-inch cubes

4 tbsp soy sauce

1 tbsp cornflour

2 garlic cloves, finely chopped

2.5-cm/1-inch piece fresh ginger, peeled and finely chopped

1 cucumber, diced, to serve

Peanut sauce

2 tbsp groundnut or vegetable oil

½ onion, finely chopped

1 garlic clove, finely chopped

4 tbsp crunchy peanut butter

4–5 tbsp water

½ tsp chilli powder

Method

1 Put the chicken cubes in a shallow dish. Mix the soy sauce, cornflour, garlic and ginger together in a small bowl and pour over the chicken. Cover and leave to marinate in the refrigerator for at least 2 hours.

2 Meanwhile, soak 12 wooden skewers in cold water for at least 30 minutes. Preheat the grill and thread the chicken pieces onto the wooden skewers. Transfer the skewers to a grill pan and cook under a preheated grill for 3–4 minutes. Turn the skewers over and cook for a further 3–4 minutes, or until cooked through. To make sure the chicken is cooked through, cut into the middle to check that there are no remaining traces of pink or red.

3 Meanwhile, to make the sauce, heat the oil in a saucepan, add the onion and garlic and cook, over a medium heat, stirring frequently, for 3–4 minutes, until softened. Add the peanut butter, water and chilli powder and simmer for 2–3 minutes, until softened and thinned. Serve the skewers immediately with the warm sauce and diced cucumber.

ROASTED MEDITERRANEAN VEGETABLE PIZZAS

Serves: 4

Prep: 50 mins, plus 1 hr rising

Cook: 30 mins

Ingredients

500 g/1 lb 2oz plum tomatoes, halved

1 red onion, cut into 8 wedges

1 aubergine, halved and sliced

2 red or orange peppers, deseeded and quartered

2 small courgettes, sliced

3 tbsp virgin olive oil

15 g/½ oz basil leaves

2 tsp balsamic vinegar

175 g/6 oz goat's cheese, crumbled

salt and pepper (optional)

1 tbsp basil leaves, to garnish

1 tbsp virgin olive oil, to serve

Pizza bases

250 g/9 oz wholemeal plain flour

½ tsp sea salt

1 tsp dark muscovado sugar

1 tsp easy-blend dried yeast

1 tbsp virgin olive oil

10 g/¼ oz wholemeal plain flour, for dusting

Method

1 Preheat the oven to 220°C/425°F/Gas Mark 7. To make the pizza bases, put the flour, salt, sugar and yeast in a mixing bowl and stir. Add the oil, then gradually mix in 150 ml/5 fl oz warm water to make a soft but not sticky dough – add more water if necessary.

2 Lightly dust a work surface with flour. Knead the dough on the surface for 5 minutes, until smooth and elastic. Return it to the bowl, cover with a clean tea-towel and put it in a warm place for 45 minutes, or until doubled in size.

3 Put the tomatoes and red onion on a baking sheet in a single layer. Put the aubergine and peppers, cut-side down, on a second baking sheet in a single layer. Put the courgettes on a third baking sheet in a single layer. Drizzle with a little oil and sprinkle with salt and pepper, if using. Roast for 15 minutes, then take out the courgettes. Roast the other two trays for 5 minutes more. Wrap the peppers in foil and leave to cool, then cut into slices.

4 Remove and discard the tomato skins, if liked, then chop the tomatoes, onion and basil and mix with the vinegar.

5 Lightly flour two baking sheets. Knead the dough, cut it into two pieces and roll out each

LUNCH

piece into an oval 30 cm/12 inches long by 15 cm/6 inches wide. Transfer them to the baking sheets, spoon over the tomato mixture, then top with the roasted vegetables. Leave to rise for 15 minutes.

Sprinkle the goat's cheese over the pizzas, then bake for 10 minutes, or until the bases are cooked and the cheese has melted. Sprinkle with oil and basil leaves. Cut each pizza into wedges and serve immediately.

Variation

Before adding the goat's cheese, stone and thinly slice 50 g/1¾ of black or green olives and sprinkle over the pizzas.

DINNER

ASPARAGUS &
EDAMAME RISOTTO

Serves: 4 **Prep: 10 mins** **Cook: 1hr 10 mins**

Ingredients

2 tbsp olive oil

1 onion, finely chopped

2 garlic cloves, crushed

1 litre/1¾ pints vegetable stock

300 g/10½ oz short-grain brown rice

400 g/14 oz asparagus

200 g/7 oz frozen edamame beans

200 g/7 oz chestnut mushrooms, sliced

125 ml/4 fl oz dry white wine

1 tbsp butter

1 tsp pepper

4 tbsp freshly grated Parmesan cheese

2 tbsp chopped fresh chervil

4 tbsp fresh Parmesan cheese shavings

salt (optional)

Method

1 Preheat the oven to 180°C/350°F/Gas Mark 4. Place a heavy, lidded flameproof casserole over a medium heat and add 1 tablespoon of the oil. Add the onion and fry, stirring frequently, for 10 minutes, or until soft and golden. Stir in the garlic.

2 Add 900 ml/1½ pints of the stock and the rice to the casserole. Stir well, bring to a simmer, then cover and bake in the centre of the preheated oven for 50 minutes, or until the rice is tender and almost all the liquid has been absorbed.

3 Meanwhile, bring a saucepan containing 5 cm/2 inches water to the boil. Add the asparagus and steam for 3 minutes, or until the spears are only just tender when pierced halfway up the stalk with a sharp knife. Rinse under cold running water, pat dry, cut into 5-cm/2-inch pieces and set aside.

4 Bring a separate small saucepan of water to the boil, add the frozen edamame beans and cook for 3 minutes, then drain and set aside.

5 Place a small frying pan over a medium–high heat and add the remaining olive oil. Add the sliced mushrooms and stir-fry for 2 minutes, then set aside.

6 Transfer the casserole to the hob and place over a medium heat. Pour in the wine and stir

DINNER

for 1 minute, then stir in the remaining stock, the butter, pepper and grated cheese. Stir for 2 minutes, or until the rice is creamy. Add a little salt to taste, if using, and stir again.

Reduce the heat to low and stir in the beans, mushrooms and chervil. Arrange the asparagus spears on top and heat through for a few minutes with the lid on. Serve the risotto immediately, sprinkled with the cheese.

Variation

You can vary this tasty risotto with any extra ingredients that you have to hand. Swap the frozen edamame beans for frozen peas and add in 350 g/12 oz cooked ham.

BUTTERNUT SQUASH LINGUINE

Serves: 2 **Prep: 15 mins** **Cook: 30 mins**

Ingredients

1 butternut squash
8 sprays cooking oil spray
2 tbsp chopped fresh
flat-leaf parsley, to garnish

Arrabbiata sauce

1 tbsp olive oil
1 onion, chopped
2 garlic cloves, crushed
1 red chilli, deseeded and
finely chopped
3 tbsp red wine
1 tsp sugar
1 tsp chilli flakes
2 tsp red pesto
200 g/7 oz canned
chopped tomatoes
4 anchovy fillets from a jar,
drained
8 black olives, stoned and
roughly chopped
1 tsp dried Italian
seasoning
½ tsp salt
½ tsp pepper

Method

1 Cut the bulbous end off the squash and set aside for another recipe. Cut the stalk off the squash and discard. Peel the remaining squash. If you are using a spiralizer, cut the squash into two chunks and put each chunk through the spiralizer. If you are using a julienne peeler, sit the squash on a stable work surface and slice off julienne strips.

2 To make the arrabbiata sauce, place a large saucepan over a medium-low heat and add the oil. Add the onion and fry for 8 minutes, or until soft and transparent. Add the garlic and chilli and stir for 1 minute. Add the wine, sugar, chilli flakes, pesto, tomatoes, anchovies, olives, Italian seasoning, salt and pepper and simmer for 20 minutes.

3 Meanwhile, preheat the oven to 190°C/375°F/ Gas Mark 5. Put the squash linguine on a large baking tray and spray with the cooking oil spray. Bake in the preheated oven for 6 minutes, and then turn the linguine over using tongs. Bake for a further 4 minutes, or until the strands are just tender with the occasional tinge of gold.

4 Transfer the linguine to warmed serving plates. Spoon the arrabbiata sauce over the linguine, garnish with the parsley and serve immediately.

DINNER

SPICY STUFFED PEPPERS WITH CHICKPEAS

Serves: 4

Prep: 10 mins, plus standing

Cook: 35 mins

Ingredients

12 sprays cooking oil spray

2 large red peppers

2 large yellow peppers

1 vegetable stock cube

85 g/3 oz bulgar wheat

125 g/4½ oz canned chickpeas, drained and rinsed

30 g/1 oz flaked almonds, toasted

30 g/1 oz raisins

4 large sun-dried tomatoes, chopped

4 spring onions, finely chopped

½ tsp smoked paprika

3 tbsp chopped fresh basil

50 g/1¾ oz feta cheese, finely crumbled

Method

1 Preheat the oven to 190°C/375°F/Gas Mark 5. Spray a baking tray with 4 sprays of cooking oil spray. Halve the red peppers and yellow peppers from stalk to base and deseed. Place cut-side down on the prepared tray and roast in the preheated oven for 20 minutes.

2 Meanwhile, prepare the bulgar wheat. Dissolve the stock cube in 175 ml/6 fl oz boiling water in a heatproof bowl and stir in the bulgar wheat. Set aside for 15 minutes, then fluff up with a fork.

3 Add the chickpeas, almonds, raisins, tomatoes, spring onion, paprika and basil to the bulgar wheat and stir well to combine.

4 Remove the peppers from the oven and stuff with the bulgar wheat mixture. Sprinkle a little cheese over the top of each stuffed pepper and spray with cooking oil spray. Roast for a further 15 minutes, or until the tops are light golden and the peppers are tender when pierced with a sharp knife. Serve immediately.

WHOLE BAKED CAULIFLOWER

Serves: 4　　　**Prep: 20–25 mins**　　**Cook: 1 hr**

Ingredients

1 tbsp olive oil

2 onions, finely sliced

4 garlic cloves, chopped

2 tbsp red wine vinegar

pinch of soft brown sugar

70 g/2½ oz black olives, stoned

2 tbsp capers

3 tbsp roughly chopped fresh basil

800 g/1 lb 12 oz canned chopped tomatoes

400 g/14 oz canned butter beans, drained and rinsed

150 ml/5 fl oz vegetable stock

1 large cauliflower, leaves trimmed

salt and pepper (optional)

2 tbsp basil sprigs, to garnish (optional)

Method

1　Heat the olive oil in a saucepan that is large enough to fit the whole cauliflower in.

2　Add the onions and garlic and fry, over a medium heat, until soft and translucent. Stir in the vinegar, brown sugar, black olives, capers and basil and heat through for a further 2–3 minutes. Pour in the tomatoes, butter beans and vegetable stock. Stir well and bring the tomato mixture to a simmer for 5–6 minutes, stirring occasionally.

3　Sit the cauliflower head upside down on a chopping board and, using a sharp knife, carefully cut the tough stem away. Place the cauliflower in the centre of the tomato sauce, pushing it down so half is covered by the sauce. Season with salt and pepper, if using.

4　Reduce the heat to low, cover and simmer for approximately 45 minutes, or until the cauliflower is tender. Carefully stir once or twice during cooking to prevent the sauce catching on the base of the pan. Serve immediately, garnished with basil, if liked.

LENTIL BURGERS

Serves: 4 **Prep: 20 mins** **Cook: 25 mins**

Ingredients

2 tsp salt

100 g/3½ oz
floury potatoes, cut into
2-cm/¾-inch cubes

100 g/3½ oz baby
spinach leaves

250 g/9 oz cooked
Puy lentils

1 onion, roughly chopped

100 g/3½ oz
chestnut mushrooms,
roughly chopped

1 heaped tbsp chopped
fresh parsley

2 tsp fresh thyme leaves

1 small egg, beaten

1½ tbsp extra virgin
rapeseed oil

To serve

4 wholemeal burger buns,
each weighing
about 50 g/1¾ oz

40 g/1½ oz
light mayonnaise

1 large tomato, sliced

240 g/8½ oz mixed
salad leaves

Method

1 Add 1 teaspoon of salt to a saucepan of water and bring to the boil. Add the potatoes, bring back to the boil and cook for 10 minutes, until soft. Drain thoroughly, then return to the hob with the heat turned off.

2 Meanwhile, put the spinach in a microwaveable bowl and microwave on High (850 watts) for 1½ minutes, or until thoroughly wilted. Transfer to a sieve and push all the moisture out using a pestle. Dry again on strong kitchen paper.

3 Put the potatoes, lentils, onion, mushrooms and 1 teaspoon of salt in a food processor and process for 1 minute to a semi-smooth mixture. Stir the spinach, parsley and thyme into the mixture by hand, then stir in the egg. Shape into four large 1-cm/½-inch thick burgers.

4 Heat the oil in a large, non-stick frying pan. Add the burgers and cook, in batches if necessary, over a medium heat for 3 minutes on each side. You may need to reduce the heat to low for the last minute of cooking on either side to prevent the burgers from overbrowning.

5 Split the burger buns and spread them with the mayonnaise. Place the burgers in the buns with the tomato slices and serve immediately with the salad leaves on the side.

DINNER

COURGETTE SPAGHETTI

Serves: 2　　　　**Prep: 30 mins**　　　　**Cook: 25–27 mins**

Ingredients

150 g/5½ oz
cherry tomatoes

4 garlic cloves, sliced

1 tbsp olive oil

50 g/1¾ oz
sunflower seeds

2 large courgettes

2 tbsp fresh pesto

70 g/2½ oz feta cheese,
crumbled

salt and pepper (optional)

25 g/1 oz fresh basil,
roughly chopped, to
garnish

Method

1 Preheat the oven to 200°C/400°F/Gas Mark 6.
Cut half of the cherry tomatoes in half and leave
the rest whole. Place all the tomatoes and sliced
garlic in a small roasting tin and drizzle over the
olive oil. Shake well to coat and place in the
preheated oven for 20 minutes.

2 Meanwhile, place a dry frying pan over a
medium heat. Add the sunflower seeds and
fry for 3–4 minutes, or until the seeds are just
toasted. Set aside.

3 To make the courgette spaghetti, lay a box
grater on its side and grate the length of the
courgette into long strands.

4 Bring a saucepan of water to the boil and
add the courgette strips. Cook for 1–2 minutes
before draining thoroughly in a colander, gently
squeezing any excess water away with the back
of a spoon. Return the spaghetti to the pan
and stir through the pesto. Season with salt and
pepper, if using.

5 Stir two thirds of the roasted tomato mixture, half
of the sunflower seeds and half of the crumbled
feta into the spaghetti and divide the mixture
between two plates. Top with the remaining
tomatoes, sunflower seeds, and feta. Garnish
with the basil. Serve immediately.

DINNER

PUMPKIN, FETA & ADUKI BEAN PARCELS

Serves: 6 **Prep: 40 mins** **Cook: 45–50 mins**

Ingredients

500 g/1 lb 2 oz pumpkin, t into 2-cm/¾-inch cubes

4 shallots, quartered

1 tsp smoked paprika

1 tbsp olive oil

200 g/7 oz canned aduki eans, drained and rinsed

2 tbsp roughly chopped fresh parsley

zest of 1 lemon

100 g/3½ oz feta cheese, crumbled

3 sheets filo pastry, each easuring 40 x 30 cm/16 x 12 inches

50 g/1¾ oz butter, melted

tbsp snipped watercress, to garnish

Method

1 Preheat the oven to 200°C/400°F/Gas Mark 6. Place the pumpkin and shallots in a shallow roasting tin in an even layer and sprinkle with the paprika. Drizzle over the olive oil and mix well. Roast in the preheated oven for 20–25 minutes. Leave the oven on. Place the pumpkin mixture in a bowl. Using a potato masher, mash until the cubes have broken down. Stir in the aduki beans, parsley, lemon zest and feta cheese. Mix until all the ingredients are well combined

2 Cut a filo sheet in half to create two long lengths of pastry (approximately 40 x 15 cm/16 x 6 inches) and brush one pastry length all over with melted butter. Cover the remaining pastry with a damp tea towel to keep it fresh.

3 Spoon a sixth of the pumpkin mixture on one end of the pastry length. Fold this edge up to meet one side to start the shape of a triangle. Fold the bottom point of the pastry up, sealing in the filling, then complete the triangle by folding again in the opposite direction. Keep folding until you reach the top and lightly brush with a little more melted butter. Repeat with the other sheets of filo until you have six triangles. Place the parcels on a baking tray and cook for 25 minutes, or until golden. Garnish with watercress and serve immediately.

DINNER

WINTER ROOT VEGETABLE TAGINE

Serves: 4   **Prep: 25 mins**   **Cook: 1 hr**

Ingredients

1 tbsp olive oil

2 red onions, thickly sliced

2 large garlic cloves, crushed

2 tbsp tomato purée

2 tbsp harissa paste

2 carrots, cut into thick batons

100 g/3½ oz potatoes, cut into 3-cm/1¼-inch chunks

200 g/7 oz sweet potatoes, cut into 3-cm/1¼-inch chunks

200 g/7 oz swede, cut into 15-mm/⅝-inch thick rounds, then quartered

600 ml/1 pint vegetable stock

150 g/5½ oz canned butter beans or cannellini beans, drained and rinsed

300 g/10½ oz canned chopped tomatoes

200 g/7 oz wholewheat couscous

large handful of fresh flat-leaf parsley, chopped

salt and pepper (optional)

Method

1 Heat the oil in a flameproof casserole, add the onions and cook over a medium–low heat for 5 minutes, or until soft and transparent. Add the garlic, tomato purée and harissa paste and cook, stirring, for 1 minute.

2 Add the carrots, potatoes, sweet potatoes and swede. Pour in the stock, add pepper, if using, and bring to a simmer. Cover and cook for 30 minutes, or until the vegetables are almost soft, stirring once halfway through.

3 Stir in the beans and tomatoes and cook for a further 15 minutes. Press some of the beans into the side of the casserole dish to break them up and thicken the sauce. Check the seasoning, adding more pepper, if using, and a pinch of salt, if using.

4 Meanwhile, prepare the couscous according to the packet instructions.

5 Scatter the parsley over the tagine and serve immediately with the couscous.

SEAFOOD STEW WITH FENNEL & PAPRIKA

Serves: 4   **Prep: 15 mins**   **Cook: 30 mins**

Ingredients

1 small fennel bulb

2 tbsp olive oil

1 large onion, finely chopped

3 garlic cloves, crushed

1 red chilli, deseeded and finely chopped

1 tsp mild paprika

pinch of saffron threads

200 ml/7 fl oz white wine

400 g/14 oz canned Italian plum tomatoes

400 ml/14 fl oz fish stock

grated zest and juice of ½ orange

3 tbsp chopped fresh flat-leaf parsley

1 tsp pepper

400 g/14 oz firm and chunky white fish fillet, cut into bite-sized pieces

200 g/7 oz ready-prepared squid, sliced

250 g/9 oz live clams

100 g/3½ oz large raw prawn tails

Method

1 Trim the fennel of its fronds, chop them and set them aside.

2 Roughly chop the fennel bulb. Place a large, deep frying pan over a medium-low heat and add the oil. Add the onion and fennel bulb and fry for 10 minutes, or until soft but not brown. Increase the heat to medium and add the garlic, chilli, paprika and saffron. Stir for a further minute, or until the spices give off their aromas.

3 Add the wine to the pan and cook for a few minutes to reduce. Tip in the tomatoes and their can juices, and the stock. Break up the tomatoes a little. Bring to a simmer and cook for 5 minutes.

4 Add the orange juice and zest, parsley and pepper to the pan. Reduce the heat to medium–low. Add the white fish, cover and simmer gently for 2–3 minutes.

5 Discard any clams that remain closed when tapped. Stir in the squid, clams and prawns and cook for a further 3 minutes, or until all the fish is cooked and the clams have opened. Discard any clams that remain closed.

6 Serve the stew in large bowls, with the fennel fronds sprinkled over the top.

DINNER

MONKFISH & PRAWN BIRYANI

Serves: 4

Prep: 15 mins, plus soaking

Cook: 35 mins

Ingredients

250 g/9 oz brown basmati rice

2½ tbsp groundnut oil

300 g/10½ oz monkfish fillet, cut into 2.5-cm/ 1-inch cubes

pinch of chilli powder

1 tsp garam masala

juice of ½ lime

200 g/7 oz raw prawns

1 large onion

1 tsp pepper

4 cloves, crushed

2 cardamom pods, crushed

½ tsp coriander seeds, lightly crushed

2 green chillies, deseeded and finely chopped

large pinch of saffron threads

½ tsp salt

1 large tomato, chopped

4 tbsp fresh coriander leaves

1 tbsp fresh mint leaves

200 ml/7 fl oz fish stock

100 ml/3½ fl oz natural yogurt

Method

1 Put the rice in a saucepan with water to cover and leave to soak for 30 minutes. Drain and rin thoroughly. Meanwhile, bring a saucepan of water to the boil, add the rice and simmer for 2 minutes, or until almost cooked. Drain thoroug

2 Place a frying pan over a high heat and add 1 tablespoon of the oil. Add the monkfish pieces sprinkle over the chilli powder and half of the garam masala and sear the fish for 1–2 minute Remove with a slotted spoon, sprinkle with half the lime juice and set aside.

3 Add the prawns to the pan and cook for 1–2 minutes, or until lightly coloured. Remove with a spoon, sprinkle with the remaining lime juice and set aside. Reduce the heat to medium.

4 Cut one half of the onion into thin slices and finely chop the other half. Add ½ tablespoon of the remaining oil to the pan, add the sliced onion and fry for 5 minutes. Increase the heat high and fry the onion slices until crisp. Remove from the pan and set aside.

5 Reduce the heat to low, add the remaining oil to the pan with the chopped onion and fry for 5 minutes, or until the onion is soft. Increase the heat to medium-high, add the pepper, cloves, cardamom, coriander seeds and chilli and stir

for 1 minute. Add the saffron, salt and the remaining garam masala and stir for 30 seconds. Stir in the chopped tomato, half of the coriander and the mint, then add the stock. Simmer for 2 minutes, then stir in the yogurt.

Tip the rice into the pan and stir to combine. Put a tight-fitting lid on the pan and cook over a very low heat for 10 minutes, or until the rice is cooked. Sprinkle in a little boiling water if the rice looks too dry before it is tender; it needs to steam inside the pan to finish cooking. Arrange the monkfish, prawns and all the plate juices over the rice, replace the lid and leave to cook for 3–5 minutes to finish cooking the fish. Meanwhile, reheat the crispy onion. Gently stir the biryani and serve immediately, topped with the crispy onion and the remaining coriander and mint leaves.

SEARED SCALLOPS WITH LIME & CHILLI SAUCE

Serves: 2　　　　**Prep: 5 mins**　　　　**Cook: 45 mins**

Ingredients

70 g/2½ oz wild rice

3 tbsp chopped fresh mixed herbs, such as parsley, tarragon, chives or dill

¼ tsp salt

½ tsp pepper

100 g/3½ oz peas

4 asparagus spears, woody ends removed

2 tsp butter

1 tbsp light olive oil

350 g/12 oz large ready-prepared scallops, thoroughly dried

3 garlic cloves, crushed

1 small red chilli, deseeded and finely chopped

juice and zest of ½ lime

2 tsp sweet chilli dipping sauce

25 g/1 oz fresh pea shoots, to garnish

Method

1 Rinse the wild rice under cold running water and drain. Bring a large saucepan of water to the boil, then add the rice. Cook for 40 minutes, or until tender, then drain thoroughly. Tip into a serving bowl and leave to cool a little. Stir in the herbs, salt and pepper.

2 Steam the peas and asparagus, with the tips of the asparagus facing upwards, for about 3–4 minutes, or until tender. Cut off the asparagus tips, set aside and keep warm. Chop the asparagus stalks and place them in a blender or food processor with the peas and the butter. Blend until smooth.

3 Brush a frying pan with a little of the oil and place over a high heat. When the pan is really hot, add the scallops. Sear for 1 minute on each side, or until golden and still soft in the centre – don't overcook or the scallops will become dry and chewy. Set aside to keep warm.

4 Reduce the heat to medium. Add the remaining oil with the garlic and chilli and stir-fry for 1 minute, or until soft. Add the lime zest and juice, then add the sweet chilli sauce and stir. Serve the scallops, drizzled with the chilli sauce, with the asparagus purée, asparagus tips and rice alongside. Garnish the scallops with the fresh pea shoots and serve immediately.

MONKFISH, MUSHROOM & RED PEPPER SKEWERS

Serves: 4   **Prep: 15 mins**   **Cook: 25 mins**

Ingredients

1 tsp salt

160 g/5¾ oz brown basmati rice

400 g/14 oz small chestnut mushrooms, stalks removed

650 g/1 lb 7 oz monkfish tail fillet

1 large red pepper, deseeded

3 back bacon rashers

1½ tbsp olive oil

5 pieces sun-dried tomato, finely chopped

1 tbsp lemon juice

1 large tomato, peeled and finely chopped

1 heaped tsp paprika

1 garlic clove, crushed

fresh coriander sprigs, to garnish

Method

1 Add the salt to a saucepan of water, add the rice, then cover and cook over a low heat for 2(minutes, or until tender but still firm to the bite.

2 Meanwhile, cut any large mushrooms in half. Cut the monkfish tail fillet into 2.5-cm/1-inch cubes and the red pepper and bacon into 2.5-cm/1-inch squares. Alternately thread the fish, mushrooms, red pepper and bacon evenly onto four metal skewers.

3 Preheat the grill and brush the kebabs with the oil. Place the kebabs on a rack under the preheated grill and cook for about 4 minutes on each side, or until the fish and bacon are cooked through and the vegetables are tender

4 To make the sauce, combine the sun-dried tomatoes, lemon juice, tomato, paprika and garlic in a small bowl.

5 Drain the rice. Serve the kebabs with the rice and a spoonful of the sauce. Garnish with coriander sprigs.

DINNER

POACHED SALMON WITH BRAISED BLACK LENTILS

Serves: 2   **Prep: 15 mins**   **Cook: 40 mins**

Ingredients

1 tbsp extra virgin rapeseed oil

shallots, finely chopped

2 garlic cloves, crushed

g/3½ oz black (Beluga) lentils

250 ml/9 fl oz vegetable stock

g/2½ oz baby spinach

¼ tsp nutmeg

juice of ¼ lemon

wild salmon fillets, each weighing 125 g/4½ oz

roughly crushed black peppercorns, to garnish

Method

1 Place a small, lidded frying pan over a medium-low heat and add the oil. Add the shallots and fry, stirring occasionally, for 5 minutes, or until soft and transparent. Add the garlic and stir for 1 minute, then stir in the lentils until coated thoroughly with the oil.

2 Add the stock to the pan, stir and bring to a simmer. Cover and cook for 20 minutes, or until the lentils are tender and most of the stock has been absorbed.

3 Stir in the spinach, nutmeg and lemon juice and cook for a further 2–3 minutes, or until the spinach wilts.

4 Meanwhile, put the salmon fillets in a shallow saucepan, cover with water and bring to a simmer. Cook for 3 minutes, or until just cooked with a hint of pink still in the centre. Drain and cut each fillet into two pieces.

5 Serve the lentils with the salmon pieces on top. Garnish with the black peppercorns and serve immediately.

TUNA WITH PAK CHOI & SOBA NOODLES

Serves: 4   **Prep: 25 mins**   **Cook: 20 mins**

Ingredients

400 g/14 oz pak choi

1 tsp salt

115 g/4 oz soba noodles

2 tuna steaks, each weighing about 175 g/6 oz

1 tbsp groundnut oil, for brushing

2 tbsp groundnut oil

2 slices fresh ginger, cut into matchsticks

½–1 fresh red chilli, deseeded and thinly sliced

4 spring onions, thickly sliced diagonally

140 g/5 oz frozen soya beans, thawed

squeeze of lime juice

3 tbsp chopped fresh coriander

Method

1 Slice the pak choi stems into bite-sized pieces. Slice the leaves into broad ribbons.

2 Add the salt to a large saucepan of water and bring to the boil. Add the noodles, bring back to the boil and cook for 5–6 minutes, until just tender. Drain, reserving the cooking water. Rinse well and set aside. Return the reserved water to the pan and keep warm over a low heat.

3 Meanwhile, cut the tuna steaks into thirds and brush with oil. Heat a ridged griddle pan over a high heat. Add the tuna and fry for 2–2½ minutes on each side. Transfer to a plate and set aside in a warm place.

4 Heat a wok over a medium–high heat. Add the oil and sizzle the ginger, chilli and spring onions for a few seconds. Add the pak choi stalks, soya beans and two tablespoons of water and stir-fry for 3 minutes. Add the pak choi leaves and stir-fry for a further minute. Add the lime juice and coriander, then season to taste with sea salt.

5 Reheat the noodles in the cooking water, then drain. Divide the noodles between two plates, add the vegetables and arrange the tuna on top. Serve immediately.

DINNER

GINGER & SESAME TROUT WITH BRAISED PAK CHOI

Serves: 2   **Prep: 10 mins**   **Cook: 10 mins**

Ingredients

2 heads of pak choi

½ tbsp groundnut oil

½ tsp Chinese five spice

2 tbsp rice wine

1 small green chilli, deseeded and finely chopped

6 sprays cooking oil spray

4 rainbow trout fillets

1 tbsp sesame oil

2 -cm/¾ -inch piece fresh ginger, finely grated

1 tbsp low-salt soy sauce

½ tbsp rice vinegar

1 tsp sesame seeds

1 tbsp ketjap manis (Indonesian soy sauce)

4 spring onions, chopped, to garnish

Method

1 Quarter each head of pak choi lengthways. Place a large saucepan over a medium–high heat and add the groundnut oil. Add the pak choi and fry for 3 minutes, or until starting to colour. Stir in the five spice and rice wine and cook for a further minute, then add 1 tablespoon of boiling water and scatter in the chopped chilli. Bring to a simmer, cover, reduce the heat to low and cook for 2–3 minutes, or until the pak choi is just tender.

2 Meanwhile, place a large frying pan over a medium–high heat and spray with 3 sprays of cooking oil spray. Add the trout fillets and cook for 2–3 minutes, then turn over with a spatula. Spray the pan with 3 sprays of cooking spray and cook for a further 2 minutes, or until the fillets are just cooked through. Remove from the pan and keep warm.

3 Reduce the heat to medium, add the sesame oil to the pan and stir in the ginger. Cook for 1 minute, then add the soy sauce, vinegar, sesame seeds and ketjap manis and stir. Serve the trout fillets with the sesame mixture spooned over the top. Garnish with the spring onions and serve with the pak choi on the side.

BAKED CHICKEN WITH PEARS & HAZELNUTS

Serves: 4　　　**Prep: 15 mins**　　　**Cook: 30 mins**

Ingredients

4 skinless chicken breast fillets, each weighing about 140 g/5 oz

1½ tbsp extra virgin rapeseed oil

4 large shallots, cut into quarters

2 small pears, peeled, cored and quartered

100 ml/3½ fl oz dry white wine

2 tsp dried oregano

2 tsp garlic purée

100 ml/3½ fl oz chicken stock

½ tsp salt

½ tsp pepper

40 g/1½ oz blanched hazelnuts, finely chopped

2 tbsp wholemeal breadcrumbs

2 tbsp chopped fresh parsley

2 tsp fresh thyme leaves

Method

1 Preheat the oven to 180°C/350°F/Gas Mark 4. Cut each of the chicken breasts into two thick steaks. Place a large frying pan over a medium heat and add 1 tablespoon of the oil. Add the shallot quarters and fry for 5 minutes, or until soft and light golden. Set aside until required.

2 Add the chicken and pears to the pan and fry over a high heat for 2–3 minutes, turning once, until light golden (you may need to do this in two batches). Arrange the chicken in a large shallow baking dish, tucking the shallots and pears around the edge.

3 Add the wine to the pan and bring to the boil. Stir in the oregano, half the garlic, all the stock and the salt and pepper. Pour the contents of the pan over the chicken mixture. Bake in the preheated oven for 15 minutes, basting the tops of the chicken pieces with the cooking juices.

4 Meanwhile, combine the hazelnuts, breadcrumbs, parsley and thyme with the remaining oil and garlic in a small bowl. Sprinkle the mixture over the top of the chicken and return to the oven for 10 minutes, or until the top has crisped a little and is lightly golden, and the chicken is tender and the juices run clear when a skewer is inserted into the thickest part of the meat. Serve immediately.

CHICKEN ESCALOPES WITH CHERRY TOMATOES

Serves: 4   **Prep: 15 mins**   **Cook: 25 mins**

Ingredients

3 skinless, boneless chicken breasts, weighing about 500 g/1 lb 2 oz in total

1 egg, beaten

100 g/3½ oz wholemeal panko breadcrumbs

1 tsp dried thyme

1 tsp dried oregano

2 tbsp groundnut oil

400 g/14 oz cherry tomatoes on the vine

200 g/7 oz baby leaf salad

1 tbsp balsamic vinegar

Method

1 Diagonally slice each chicken breast in four lengthways to make 12 escalopes. Place each escalope on a chopping board and pound it a few times with a rolling pin to a thickness of about 1 cm/½ inch.

2 Put the beaten egg in a shallow dish and put the breadcrumbs in a separate shallow dish. Stir the thyme and oregano into the breadcrumbs.

3 Coat each escalope in egg, allowing the excess to drip off. Dip into the breadcrumb mixture, turning to coat, then transfer to a large plate.

4 Heat the oil in a large, non-stick frying pan. Add the escalopes, in batches, and cook over a medium heat for about 4 minutes on each side, until the breadcrumbs are golden and the escalopes are cooked through.

5 Meanwhile, preheat the grill and grill the tomatoes on the vine until warmed through but not collapsed.

6 Serve the escalopes with the grilled tomatoes and the baby leaf salad, drizzled with the balsamic vinegar.

JERK CHICKEN WITH PAPAYA & AVOCADO SALSA

Serves: 4   **Prep: 35 mins**   **Cook: 30–35 mins**

Ingredients

1 tsp allspice berries, crushed

1 tsp coriander seeds, crushed

1 tsp mild paprika

¼ tsp freshly grated nutmeg

1 tbsp fresh thyme leaves

1 tbsp black peppercorns, coarsely crushed

pinch of salt

1 kg/2 lb 4 oz small chicken drumsticks, skinned

1 tbsp olive oil

Salsa

1 papaya, halved, deseeded, peeled and cut into cubes

2 large avocados, stoned, peeled and cut into cubes

finely grated zest and juice of 1 lime

½ red chilli, deseeded and finely chopped

½ red onion, finely chopped

15 g/½ oz fresh coriander, finely chopped

2 tsp chia seeds

Method

1 Preheat the oven to 200°C/400°F/Gas Mark 6. To make the jerk spice rub, mix together the allspice berries, coriander seeds, paprika, nutmeg, thyme leaves, peppercorns and salt in a small bowl.

2 Slash each chicken drumstick two or three times with a knife, then put them in a roasting tin and drizzle with the oil. Sprinkle the spice mix over the chicken, then rub it in with your fingers, washing your hands well afterwards.

3 Roast the chicken for 30–35 minutes, or until browned with piping hot juices that run clear with no sign of pink when a knife is inserted into the thickest part of a drumstick.

4 Meanwhile, to make the salsa, put the papaya and avocados in a bowl, sprinkle over the lime zest and juice, then toss well. Add the chilli, red onion, coriander and chia seeds and stir.

5 Serve immediately.

DINNER

HARISSA CHICKEN IN PITTAS WITH FREEKEH

Serves: 2

Prep: 10 mins,
plus marinating

Cook: 10 mins

Ingredients

2 small skinless chicken breast fillets, each weighing about 115 g/4 oz

juice of 1 lime

1½ tsp harissa paste

½ tbsp olive oil

1 tsp sesame seeds

1 tsp dried oregano

1 tsp sumac

1 tsp ground cumin

¼ tsp ground cinnamon

½ tsp salt

½ tsp pepper

3 tbsp Greek-style yogurt

100 g/3½ oz cooked freekeh

1 large tomato, finely diced

30 g/1 oz red onion, finely diced

6 -cm/2½ -inch piece cucumber, deseeded and finely diced

2 tbsp fresh coriander leaves

2 wholemeal pittas

4 lettuce leaves, torn

Method

1 Cut the chicken into bite-sized pieces and put them into a non-metallic shallow dish. Combine half the lime juice with the harissa paste and o[i]l. Add to the dish and toss the chicken thoroughl[y] in the mixture. Cover and set aside for up to 1 hour to marinate.

2 Combine the sesame seeds, oregano, sumac, cumin, cinnamon, salt and pepper in a small bowl. Stir half of the spice mixture into the yogu[rt.] Combine the freekeh with the tomato, onion, cucumber, coriander and the remaining spice mixture and lime juice.

3 Preheat the grill to medium–high. Place the marinated chicken pieces on a grill pan lined with foil and cook about 5 cm/2 inches away from the heat source. After 3 minutes, or when the chicken is beginning to brown, turn the pieces over and cook for a further 3 minutes, or until the chicken pieces are cooked throug[h] and the coating is nicely browned.

4 Warm the pittas, then fill with the chicken, lettuc[e] and yogurt. Serve immediately, with the freekeh salad on the side.

HEALTHY SPAGHETTI BOLOGNESE

Serves: 4   **Prep: 15 mins**   **Cook: 45 mins**

Ingredients

1 tbsp rapeseed oil

1 large onion, finely chopped

2 celery sticks, finely chopped

3 garlic cloves, crushed

1 large carrot, finely chopped

500 g/1 lb 2 oz fresh turkey mince

400 g/14 oz canned chopped tomatoes

125 g/4½ oz chestnut mushrooms, finely chopped

1 tbsp tomato purée

200 ml/7 fl oz fat-free turkey gravy

1 tsp instant gravy granules

2 tsp Italian seasoning

1–2 tsp salt

300 g/10½ oz dried wholegrain spelt spaghetti

2 tbsp grated Parmesan cheese

Method

1 Place a large, lidded frying pan over a medium-low heat and add the oil. Add the onion and celery and fry, covered, stirring occasionally, for 10 minutes, or until soft and transparent. Stir in the garlic and carrot and cook for a further minute. Push all of the vegetables to the edge of the pan and add the mince to the centre. Increase the heat to medium–high and cook, stirring occasionally, for 2–3 minutes, or until the mince is brown all over.

2 Stir in the tomatoes, mushrooms, tomato purée, gravy, gravy granules and Italian seasoning. Bring to a simmer, reduce the heat to low, cover and cook as gently as you can for 30 minutes, stirring occasionally. Check that all the vegetables are cooked before serving.

3 Meanwhile, add 1–2 teaspoons of salt to a large saucepan of water and bring to the boil. Add the spaghetti and cook for 10 minutes, or until tender but still firm to the bite. Drain the spaghetti and serve in warmed bowls with the sauce spooned over the top, sprinkled with the Parmesan cheese.

DINNER

SPICED TURKEY STEW WITH WHOLEGRAIN COUSCOUS

Serves: 4   **Prep: 20 mins**   **Cook: 25 mins**

Ingredients

1 tbsp virgin olive oil

500 g/1 lb 2 oz skinless and boneless turkey breast, cut into 2-cm/¾-inch pieces

1 onion, roughly chopped

2 garlic cloves, finely chopped

1 red pepper, deseeded and roughly chopped

1 orange pepper, deseeded and roughly chopped

500 g/1 lb 2 oz tomatoes, roughly chopped

1 tsp cumin seeds, roughly crushed

1 tsp paprika

finely grated zest and juice of 1 unwaxed lemon

salt and pepper (optional)

To serve

200 g/7 oz wholegrain giant couscous

2 tbsp roughly chopped fresh flat-leaf parsley

2 tbsp roughly chopped fresh coriander

Method

1 Heat the oil in a large frying pan over a medium heat. Add the turkey, a few pieces at a time, then add the onion. Fry, stirring, for 5 minutes, or until the turkey is golden.

2 Add the garlic, red and orange peppers and tomatoes, then stir in the cumin seeds and paprika. Add the lemon juice and season with salt and pepper, if using. Stir well, then cover and cook, stirring from time to time, for 20 minutes, or until the tomatoes have formed a thick sauce and the turkey is cooked through and the juices run clear with no sign of pink when a piece is cut in half.

3 Meanwhile, half-fill a saucepan with water and bring to the boil. Add the couscous and cook according to the packet instructions, or until just tender. Tip into a sieve and drain well.

4 Spoon the couscous onto plates and top with the turkey stew. Mix the parsley and coriander with the lemon zest, then sprinkle over the stew and serve.

BLACK BEAN PORK WITH CAULIFLOWER RICE

Serves: 4   **Prep: 15 mins**   **Cook: 35 mins**

Ingredients

500 g/1 lb 2 oz lean pork fillet, sliced

3 tbsp low-salt soy sauce

1 large head of cauliflower, cut into florets

1 large red pepper, halved and deseeded

2½ tbsp groundnut oil

4 large spring onions, diagonally sliced

1 onion, finely chopped

2 garlic cloves, crushed

4 -cm/1½ -inch piece fresh ginger, grated

1 red chilli, deseeded and finely chopped

100 g/3½ oz canned black beans, drained, rinsed and lightly crushed

1 tbsp brown sugar

125 ml/4 fl oz chicken stock

1½ tsp cornflour

1 tsp crushed cumin seeds

4 tbsp fresh coriander leaves

Method

1 Place the pork slices in a non-metallic shallow dish. Sprinkle over 1 tablespoon of the soy sauce, stir to coat, then cover and set aside.

2 Place the cauliflower florets in a food processor or chopper. Pulse (in two or three batches if necessary) until they resemble grains of rice; do not over-process. Tip the cauliflower into a bowl and set aside.

3 Finely chop one half of the red pepper and cut the other half into thin strips. Place a large covered frying pan over a high heat and add ½ tablespoon of the oil. Add the sliced red pepper and spring onions and fry for 3 minutes, until lightly charred and soft. Remove with a slotted spatula and keep warm. Add ½ tablespoon of the remaining oil to the pan, add the pork slices and fry for 1 minute on each side, until turning golden. Remove from the pan with the slotted spatula, set aside and keep warm.

4 Add ½ tablespoon of the remaining oil to the pan and reduce the heat to medium–low. Add the onion and chopped red pepper and fry for 10 minutes, or until soft and transparent. Stir in the garlic, ginger and chilli.

5 Add the beans to the pan with the remaining soy sauce, the sugar and stock. Stir well, cover

and simmer for 5 minutes. Add the pork slices to the pan and simmer for a further 5 minutes, or until the slices are cooked through. Stir in the cornflour to thicken the sauce. If the sauce is too thick for your liking, add a little hot water to thin.

6 Place a small frying pan over a medium heat and add the remaining oil. Add the cauliflower rice to the pan with the crushed cumin seeds. Stir well, then cover and cook, stirring occasionally, for 5 minutes, or until the cauliflower is cooked but is still firm to the bite.

7 Serve the cauliflower on warmed serving plates and top with the pork mixture. Sprinkle over the spring onions, red pepper slices and coriander and serve immediately.

PORK MEDALLIONS WITH POMEGRANATE

Serves: 4 **Prep: 20 mins** **Cook: 40–45 mins**

Ingredients

150 g/5½ oz wheatberries

25 g/1 oz fresh flat-leaf parsley, roughly chopped

55 g/2 oz kale, shredded

seeds of 1 pomegranate

500 g/1 lb 2 oz pork medallions

1 tbsp olive oil

2 garlic cloves, finely chopped

Dressing

50 g/1¾ oz walnuts, roughly chopped

3 tbsp virgin olive oil

3 tsp pomegranate molasses

juice of 1 lemon

Method

1 Bring a medium saucepan of water to the boil. Add the wheatberries and simmer for 25–30 minutes, or until tender. Drain and rinse.

2 Meanwhile, to make the dressing, put the walnuts in a large frying pan and toast for 2–3 minutes, or until just beginning to brown. Put the virgin olive oil, the pomegranate molasses and lemon juice in a small bowl and mix together with a fork. Stir in the hot walnuts.

3 Mix together the parsley, kale and pomegranate seeds in a large bowl.

4 Remove the visible fat from the pork. Heat the olive oil in the frying pan over a medium heat. Add the pork and garlic and fry for 10 minutes, turning halfway through, until browned and cooked. Cut into the centre of one of the pork medallions; any juices that run out should be clear and piping hot with steam rising. Slice the pork into strips.

5 Add the wheatberries to the kale mixture and gently toss. Transfer to a platter, pour over the dressing, then top with the pork.

DINNER

BLACK RICE RISOTTO WITH PARMA HAM

Serves: 4   **Prep: 10 mins**   **Cook: 1 hr**

Ingredients

200 g/7 oz black rice

1 tsp sea salt

6 Parma ham slices

1 tbsp olive oil

2 small heads chicory, quartered lengthways

15 g/½ oz butter

garlic cloves, thinly sliced

1 small shallot, roughly chopped

500 ml/17 fl oz chicken stock

sp mascarpone cheese

2 tbsp roughly chopped fresh flat-leaf parsley

Method

1 Cook the rice in a large pan of boiling water with the salt for 45 minutes, or until tender but slightly chewy.

2 Heat a deep frying pan over a medium–high heat. Add the Parma ham and dry-fry for 30 seconds on each side, or until crisp. Transfer to a plate.

3 Add the oil to the pan, then fry the chicory for 2 minutes on each side, or until darkly golden. Remove from the pan, wrap in kitchen foil to keep warm and set aside.

4 Reduce the heat to medium, then melt the butter in the pan. Add the garlic and shallot and fry for 4 minutes, or until softened. Add the cooked and drained rice and stock, bring to a simmer, then cook gently for 5 minutes, or until two-thirds of the liquid has been absorbed. Stir in the mascarpone and parsley, then return the chicory to the pan and warm through.

5 Crumble the Parma ham into large shards. Serve the risotto heaped into four bowls with the crisp ham on top.

PORK MEATBALLS
IN CHILLI BROTH

Serves: 4

Prep: 30 mins,
plus chilling

Cook: 30 mins

Ingredients

1.2 litres/2 pints
chicken stock

¼–½ fresh red chilli,
deseeded and
very finely sliced

½ tsp palm sugar or
soft light brown sugar

3 fresh thyme sprigs

2 lemon grass stalks,
fibrous outer leaves
removed, stems bashed
with the flat of a knife

1 small head pak choi,
stems cut into small
squares, leaves sliced
into ribbons

1 spring onion, green parts
included, sliced diagonally

1 tsp soy sauce

salt and pepper (optional)

Pork meatballs

225 g/8 oz fresh pork mince

1 shallot, grated

2-cm/¾-inch piece fresh
ginger, crushed

1 garlic clove, crushed

finely grated zest
and juice of ½ lime

6 tbsp groundnut oil

salt and pepper (optional)

Method

1 Pour the stock into a medium-sized saucepan.
Add the chilli, sugar, thyme, lemon grass, a good
pinch of pepper, and salt to taste, if using, and
bring to the boil. Reduce the heat and simmer
gently for 10 minutes. Remove from the heat and
leave to cool for about 30 minutes.

2 To make the meatballs, combine the pork,
shallot, ginger, garlic, lime zest and juice, and
season with salt and pepper, if using. Mix well
with a fork. Line a plate with kitchen paper.

3 Divide the mixture into 16–20 walnut-sized balls.
Place on the prepared plate and chill for 30
minutes.

4 Heat a large wok over a high heat. Add the oil
and heat until very hot. Add the pork meatballs
and fry for 5–6 minutes, until golden brown all
over and cooked through. Drain on kitchen
paper and keep warm.

5 Remove the thyme and lemon grass from the
broth. Add the pak choi and spring onion. Bring
to the boil then simmer for 2 minutes until the
pak choi stalks are just tender. Season with soy
sauce. Ladle the broth and vegetables over the
meatballs in bowls and serve immediately.

SPICY STEAK WITH ROASTED SQUASH

Serves: 4   **Prep: 20–30 mins**   **Cook: 35–40 mins**

Ingredients

750 g/1 lb 10 oz butternut squash, cut into chunks

4 garlic cloves, finely chopped

4 large portobello mushrooms, cut into thick slices

15 g/½ oz finely chopped fresh sage, leaves only

4 tbsp olive oil

4 x 175 g/6 oz fillet steaks

salt and pepper (optional)

Chimichurri sauce

30 g/1 oz fresh flat-leaf parsley

½ tsp dried oregano

2 garlic cloves

1 shallot, chopped

¼ tsp dried chilli flakes

grated zest and juice of ½ lemon

2 tbsp red wine vinegar

2 tbsp olive oil

2 tbsp cold water

Method

1 Preheat the oven to 200°C/400°F/Gas Mark 6. Place the squash, garlic, mushrooms and sage in a large roasting tin. Drizzle over 2 tablespoons of olive oil and mix well. Season with salt and pepper, if using, and roast in the preheated oven for 25–30 minutes, turning once halfway through the cooking time.

2 Meanwhile, make the sauce. Place all of the ingredients, except the water, in a bowl and blend using a hand-held blender or food processor. Carefully pour in the water, adding just enough to reach a spooning consistency. Set aside.

3 Brush the steaks with 1 tablespoon of olive oil and season with salt and pepper, if using. Place a heavy frying pan or griddle over a high heat and once smoking, add the steaks and reduce the heat to medium–high. Cook for 2–3 minutes on each side for medium–rare, or cook to your taste. Remove the steaks from the pan and leave them to rest for a few minutes before serving.

4 Cut the steaks into thick slices and serve on top of the roasted vegetables. Drizzle over the chimichurri sauce and 1 tablespoon of olive oil.

DINNER

LEAN BEEFSTEAKS WITH SPICY BEAN CAKES

Serves: 2 **Prep: 15 mins** **Cook: 15 mins**

Ingredients

1 small sweet potato, weighing about 100 g/3½ oz

½ tbsp olive oil

1 small red onion, finely chopped

2 garlic cloves, crushed

1 green chilli, deseeded and finely chopped

200 g/7 oz canned mixed beans, drained and rinsed

2 tbsp fresh breadcrumbs

1 egg yolk

¼ tsp cayenne pepper

1 tsp pepper

½ tsp salt

2 sirloin steaks, fat band removed, each weighing about 150 g/5½ oz

6 sprays cooking oil spray

Method

1 Prick the skin of the sweet potato with a fork and cook in the microwave on High for 5 minutes, or until just tender. Leave to cool for a few minutes. Meanwhile, place a frying pan over a medium heat and add the oil. Add the onion and fry for 8 minutes, or until soft. Add the garlic and chilli to the pan and fry for a further minute.

2 Mash the beans in a bowl until you have a smooth consistency with a few lumps. Use a slotted spatula to remove the onion mixture from the pan and stir into the beans. Halve the sweet potato, scoop out the flesh, and add to the bean mixture with the breadcrumbs, egg yolk, cayenne pepper, pepper and salt. Mix well to combine and shape into four flat round cakes.

3 Reheat the pan, which should still have a thin layer of oil coating it, over a medium heat. Add the bean cakes and cook for approximately 3 minutes on each side, or until nicely golden. Meanwhile, place a ridged griddle pan over a high heat. Spray the steaks with the cooking oil spray and, when the pan is very hot, add the steaks and cook for 1½ minutes on each side for rare, or to your liking. Leave to rest for a few minutes, then serve with the bean cakes and any juices that have come from the steaks.

DINNER

SLOW-COOKED BEEF WITH SMASHED BUTTER BEANS

Serves: 6 | **Prep: 30 mins** | **Cook: 4 hrs 15 mins –4 hrs 45 mins**

Ingredients

2 tbsp olive oil

1.6 kg/3 lb 8 oz beef brisket

4 onions, sliced

2 garlic cloves, crushed

1 tbsp tomato purée

1 kg/2 lb 4 oz ripe tomatoes, cut into quarters

750 ml/1¼ pints beef stock

salt and pepper (optional)

2 tbsp roughly chopped fresh parsley, to garnish

Smashed butter beans

1 tbsp olive oil

3 shallots, finely chopped

3 garlic cloves, finely sliced

1 fresh rosemary sprig, finely chopped

800 g/1 lb 12 oz canned butter beans, drained and rinsed

zest and juice of 1 lemon

Method

1 Place a 6-litre/10½-pint flameproof casserole dish over a high heat. Add the olive oil and, using tongs to hold the meat, brown the beef all over. Set the beef aside. Reduce the heat slightly and add the onions and garlic.

2 Cook for 4–5 minutes, or until the onion and garlic have softened. Stir in the tomato purée. Add the fresh tomatoes and continue to cook for 1–2 minutes.

3 Return the beef to the casserole dish and nestle the beef in the centre of the pot. Pour the stock around the beef. Season with salt and pepper, if using.

4 Reduce the heat to low. Partially cover the dish, allowing just a little steam to escape, and cook for 4–4½ hours, stirring regularly to prevent the bottom of the saucepan sticking. Top up with a little cold water if you think the pot is looking dry. The beef should be tender and easily torn apart with a knife and fork.

5 Meanwhile, to make the smashed butter beans, heat the oil in a large frying pan and fry the shallots, garlic and rosemary for 3–4 minutes, or until the shallots are soft. Stir in the drained butter beans with 200 ml/7 fl oz water.

Bring to a simmer and cook for 5 minutes, or until the butter beans are softened. Gently mash the butter beans, stirring through the zest and juice of the lemon. Serve immediately, garnished with the chopped parsley.

Variation

Serve with carrot mash. Preheat the oven to 200°C/400°F/Gas Mark 6. Place 1.25 kg/2 lb 12 oz of carrots, cut in half lengthways, in a roasting tin. Add 1 teaspoon each of turmeric, coriander and cumin. Drizzle over 2 tablespoons of olive oil and mix well. Roast in the preheated oven for 35 minutes until soft. Remove and cool slightly, then firmly mash.

DESSERTS & BAKING

RASPBERRY RICOTTA CHEESECAKE

Serves: 8

Prep: 40 mins, plus chilling

Cook: 15 mins

Ingredients

1 tbsp virgin olive oil, to grease

25 g/1 oz unsalted butter

1 tbsp virgin olive oil

6 tbsp maple syrup

40 g/1½ oz porridge oats

40 g/1½ oz unblanched almonds, roughly chopped

40 g/1½ oz unblanched hazelnuts, roughly chopped

finely grated zest of ¼ unwaxed lemon, to decorate

8 tsp maple syrup, for drizzling

Topping

4 tbsp cold water

2½ tsp powdered gelatine

250 g/9 oz ricotta cheese

250 g/9 oz mascarpone cheese

250 g/9 oz natural yogurt

finely grated zest and juice of 1 unwaxed lemon

150 g/5½ oz raspberries

Method

1 To make the base, preheat the oven to 160°C/325°F/Gas Mark 3. Brush a 23-cm/9-inch diameter round non-stick springform baking tin with a little oil.

2 Put the butter, oil and 2 tablespoons of maple syrup in a saucepan over a medium–low heat until the butter has melted. Remove the pan from the heat and stir in the oats and nuts.

3 Tip the mixture into the prepared tin and press down into an even layer with the back of a fork. Bake for 15 minutes, or until golden, then leave to cool.

4 To make the topping, spoon the water into a small heatproof bowl, then sprinkle the gelatine over the top, making sure all the powder is absorbed. Soak for 5 minutes. Place the bowl over a saucepan of gently simmering water until you have a clear liquid.

5 Put the ricotta, mascarpone and yogurt in a bowl, spoon in the remaining 4 tablespoons of maple syrup and whisk until smooth.

6 Mix in the lemon zest and juice, then gradually whisk in the gelatine mixture. Add half the raspberries and crush them into the mixture with a fork.

DESSERTS & BAKING

Spoon the topping onto the base and smooth the surface, then sprinkle with the remaining raspberries. Cover the cheesecake and chill in the refrigerator for 4–6 hours, or until set.

To serve, run a knife around the edge of the tin, release the side and slide the cheesecake onto a serving plate. Decorate with the remaining lemon zest, cut into wedges and drizzle with extra maple syrup.

Variation

Swap the raspberries for blackberries and make the cheesecake in the same way. Instead of drizzling with maple syrup, try honey for extra vitamins.

TOFU LEMON CHEESECAKE

Serves: 10

Prep: 35–40 mins, **Cook: 5 mins**
plus chilling

Ingredients

Base

125 g/4½ oz pecan nuts

175 g/6 oz soft dried dates

85 g/3 oz gingernut biscuits

2 tbsp agave syrup

1 tbsp lemon zest, to decorate

Filling

350 g/12 oz firm silken tofu

300 g/10½ oz full-fat cream cheese

100 g/3½ oz Greek-style natural yogurt

grated zest and juice of 3 lemons

100 g/3½ oz soft light brown sugar

½ tsp vanilla extract

15 g/½ oz powdered gelatine

75 ml/2½ fl oz cold water

Method

1 Line a 20-cm/8-inch round springform baking ti with baking paper.

2 To make the base, place the pecans, dates, biscuits and agave syrup in a food processor and pulse until the mixture comes together. The mixture should be slightly sticky when rolled in your hands. Tip the mixture into the prepared tir and press down to create an even base.

3 To make the filling, drain any excess water from the tofu and place in a food processor with the cream cheese, yogurt, lemon zest, lemon juice brown sugar and vanilla extract. Blend until silk smooth.

4 Place the powdered gelatine in a small bowl and pour over the cold water. Set the bowl over a saucepan of gently simmering water. Stir the gelatine until it has dissolved into the liquid and working quickly, pour the liquid gelatine into the filling mixture. Blend the filling again until the gelatine is fully incorporated.

5 Spoon the filling on top of the base and place in the refrigerator to chill for 6 hours or overnigh Serve in slices, decorated with the lemon zest.

GRILLED STONE FRUIT POTS

Serves: 6   **Prep: 10 mins**   **Cook: 5 mins**

Ingredients

375 g/13 oz low-fat ricotta cheese

2 tsp finely grated orange zest

3 peaches, stoned and quartered

3 nectarines, stoned and quartered

3 plums or apricots, stoned and quartered

2 tbsp honey, ideally orange-blossom

2 tbsp flaked almonds

Method

1 Preheat the grill to medium–high. Line the grill rack with foil.

2 Put the ricotta cheese and orange zest in a bowl and stir well.

3 Lay all the fruit in a single layer on the foil-lined grill rack. Grill, turning halfway, for 5 minutes, or until softened and beginning to caramelize.

4 Spoon the ricotta into six glasses. Top each with some fruit, drizzle with the honey and sprinkle with the flaked almonds. Serve immediately.

COCONUT RICE PUDDING WITH POMEGRANATE

Serves: 4

Prep: 15 mins, plus chilling

Cook: 45–50 mins

Ingredients

55 g/2 oz pudding rice

200 ml/7 fl oz canned light coconut milk

200 ml/7 fl oz almond milk

25 g/1 oz golden caster sugar

1 cinnamon stick

2 gelatine leaves

1 pomegranate, separated into seeds

¼ tsp grated nutmeg, to sprinkle

Method

1 Place the rice, coconut milk, almond milk, sugar and cinnamon in a saucepan over a high heat. Bring almost to the boil, stirring, then reduce the heat and cover. Simmer very gently, stirring occasionally, for 40–45 minutes, or until most of the liquid is absorbed

2 Meanwhile, place the gelatine leaves in a bowl and cover with cold water. Leave to soak for 10 minutes to soften. Drain the leaves, squeezing out any excess moisture, then add to the hot rice mixture and stir lightly until the gelatine has completely dissolved.

3 Spoon the rice mixture into four 150-ml/5-fl oz metal pudding basins, spreading evenly. Leave to cool, then cover and chill in the refrigerator until firm.

4 Run a small knife around the edge of each basin. Dip the bases briefly into a bowl of hot water, then turn out the rice onto four plates.

5 Scatter the pomegranate seeds over the rice, then sprinkle with grated nutmeg. Serve immediately.

SUMMER PAVLOVA

Serves: 6

Prep: 20 mins,
plus chilling

**Cook: 1 hr 30 mins
~2 hrs**

Ingredients

Meringue
2 egg whites
40 g/1½ oz caster sugar
1 tsp cornflour
1 tsp vanilla extract
1 tsp vinegar

Filling
200 g/7 oz low-fat cream
cheese
150 g/5½ oz low-fat natural
yogurt
½–1 tsp vanilla extract,
or to taste
300 g/10½ oz
mixed berries

Method

1 Preheat the oven to 120°C/250°F/Gas Mark ½ and line a baking sheet with baking paper. To make the meringue, whisk the egg whites in a large, grease-free bowl until stiff then gradually add the sugar a spoonful at a time, whisking well after each addition. Stir in the cornflour, vanilla extract and the vinegar.

2 When all the sugar has been added and the mixture is stiff, spoon onto the lined baking sheet and form into a 15-cm/6-inch round, hollowing out the centre to form a case.

3 Bake in the preheated oven for 1½–2 hours, or until crisp. Switch the oven off and leave to cool in the oven. Remove from the oven and leave until cold before removing from the baking sheet. Store the meringue in an airtight container until required.

4 To make the filling, beat the cream cheese and yogurt together in a bowl until well blended, then stir in the vanilla extract. Cut any large fruits into bite-sized pieces. When ready to serve, pile the cream cheese filling in the centre of the pavlova case, top with the fruits and serve, cut into six pieces.

COFFEE ICE CREAM

Serves: 6

Prep: 15 mins, plus freezing

Cook: No cooking

Ingredients

25 g/1 oz plain chocolate

225 g/8 oz ricotta cheese

5 tbsp low-fat natural yogurt

85 g/3 oz caster sugar

175 ml/6 fl oz strong black coffee, cooled and chilled

½ tsp ground cinnamon

dash of vanilla extract

25 g/1 oz plain chocolate flakes, to decorate

Method

1 Grate the chocolate and reserve. Place the ricotta cheese, yogurt and sugar in a blender or food processor and process until smooth. Transfer to a large bowl and beat in the coffee, cinnamon, vanilla extract and grated chocolate.

2 Spoon the mixture into a freezerproof container and freeze for 1½ hours, or until slushy. Remove from the freezer, turn into a bowl and beat. Return to the container and freeze for 1½ hours.

3 Repeat this beating and freezing process twice more before serving in scoops, decorated with chocolate flakes. Alternatively, leave in the freezer until 15 minutes before serving, then transfer to the refrigerator to soften slightly before scooping into bowls.

DESSERTS & BAKING

RAW CHOCOLATE ICE CREAM

Prep: 15 mins,
plus freezing

Cook: No cooking

Ingredients

...nanas, about
...½ oz, peeled
... unsweetened
...ocoa powder

1 tbsp agave nectar

Method

1 Cut the bananas into 2-cm/¾-inch pieces. Place them in a freezer bag and freeze for 3 hours.

2 Put the frozen bananas in a food processor or blender. Add the cocoa powder and agave nectar and process until smooth. Scoop and serve immediately or refreeze for a firmer consistency.

RASPBERRY & WATERMELON SORBET

Serves: 4

Prep: 30 mins,
plus cooling & freezing

Cook: 7–9 mins

Ingredients

115 g/4 oz golden
caster sugar

150 ml/5 fl oz cold water

finely grated zest
and juice of 1 lime

225 g/8 oz raspberries

1 small watermelon,
deseeded, peeled and
cut into chunks

1 egg white

Method

1 Put the sugar, water and lime zest in a small saucepan and cook over a low heat, stirring, until the sugar has dissolved. Increase to high until the mixture comes to the boil, then reduce the heat to medium and simmer for 3–4 minutes. Leave the syrup to cool completely.

2 Put the raspberries and watermelon in a food processor in batches and process to a purée, then press through a sieve into a bowl to remove any remaining seeds.

3 Tip the purée into a loaf tin, pour in the lime syrup through a sieve, then stir in the lime juice. Freeze for 3–4 hours, or until the sorbet is beginning to freeze around the edges and the centre is still mushy.

4 Transfer the sorbet to a food processor and process to break up the ice crystals. Put the egg white in a small bowl and lightly whisk with a fork until frothy, then mix it into the sorbet.

5 Pour the sorbet into a plastic or metal container, cover and freeze for 3–4 hours, or until firm. Allow to soften at room temperature for 10 minutes before serving.

PINEAPPLE CARPACCIO WITH MANGO SAUCE

Serves: 4　　　　　**Prep: 10 mins**　　　　　**Cook: No cooking**

Ingredients

1 small pineapple
1 ripe mango
juice of ½ lime
100 g/3½ oz fat-free natural yogurt

Method

1 Trim the top and base from the pineapple, then cut off all the skin and remove the 'eyes'. Use a large sharp knife to slice the pineapple into very thin slices. Arrange the slices overlapping on a wide platter.

2 Peel, stone and chop the mango flesh, then sprinkle with lime juice and use a hand-held blender or food processor to process to a smooth purée.

3 Place the mango purée in a small bowl. Swirl in the yogurt and swirl to create a marbled effect.

4 Place the bowl of mango sauce in the centre of the platter. Serve the pineapple with the sauce spooned over.

CRUNCH-TOPPED ROAST PEARS

Serves: 4 **Prep: 10 mins** **Cook: 20 mins**

Ingredients

4 dessert pears, such as Comice or Bartlett, each weighing about 150 g/5½ oz

200 ml/7 fl oz medium white wine

1 tbsp demerara sugar

½ tsp ground mixed spice

25 g/1 oz mixed nuts, toasted and chopped

15 g/½ oz rolled oats

2 tbsp wholemeal breadcrumbs

2 tsp sunflower seeds

8 sprays of cooking oil spray

Method

1 Preheat the oven to 190°C/375°F/Gas Mark 5.

2 Cut the pears in half lengthways and remove the cores. Place in a large shallow baking dish. Pour the white wine around the pears and bake in the preheated oven for 10 minutes.

3 Meanwhile, combine the sugar, spice, nuts, oats, breadcrumbs and sunflower seeds in a bowl.

4 Remove the pears from the oven, top each with some of the nut mixture, then spray with cooking oil spray. Return to the oven for 7–8 minutes, or until the topping is golden. Serve drizzled with any juice left in the dish.

HEALTHY APPLE CRUMBLE

Serves: 6

Prep: 25 mins,
plus chilling

Cook: 40–45 mins

Ingredients

800 g/1 lb 12 oz cooking apples, peeled, cored and chopped into 2-cm/¾-inch chunks

¼ tsp ground cloves

¼ tsp ground cinnamon

1 tsp ground ginger

3 tbsp brown sugar

Topping

200 g/7 oz rolled oats

½ tsp ground cinnamon

3 tbsp runny honey

3 tbsp coconut oil, at room temperature

50 g/1¾ oz macadamia nuts, roughly chopped

2 tbsp demerara sugar

Method

1 Preheat the oven to 180°C/350°F/Gas Mark 4.

2 Place the apple chunks in a large saucepan. Add 2 tablespoons of cold water, the cloves, cinnamon, ginger and brown sugar and place over a medium heat. Stew for about 15 minutes, stirring regularly, or until the apples begin to just lose their shape. Put the apples into a 1.2-litre/2-pint baking dish.

3 To make the topping, simply place the oats in a medium bowl. Stir in the cinnamon, honey, coconut oil, macadamia nuts and sugar and mix well.

4 Sprinkle the topping mixture over the stewed apple and bake for 25–30 minutes, or until golden. Remove from the oven and leave to cool for a few minutes before serving.

CHOCOLATE & CHIA PUDDINGS

Serves: 3

Prep: 20 mins, plus chilling

Cook: No cooking

Ingredients

2 tbsp cocoa powder

2 tbsp agave syrup

90 ml/3 fl oz coconut milk

125 g/4½ oz Greek-style natural yogurt

2 tbsp chia seeds

1 tsp vanilla extract

1 kiwi, sliced, to decorate

50 g/1¾ oz plain chocolate, roughly chopped, to decorate

Method

1 Place the cocoa powder and agave syrup in a large bowl and mix well to remove any lumps. Stir in the coconut milk, Greek yogurt, chia seeds and vanilla extract and mix thoroughly.

2 Cover and refrigerate for 4–6 hours. Remove the mixture from the refrigerator; it should be quite thick at this stage. Using an electric hand-held blender, whizz the mixture until smooth and divide among three small dessert glasses.

3 Chill the puddings for a further hour. Decorate with the kiwi slices and chocolate and serve.

FROZEN YOGURT CUPS

Makes: 12

Prep: 10 mins,
plus freezing

Cook: No cooking

Ingredients

450 g/1 lb low-fat
natural yogurt

1½ tbsp finely grated
orange zest

225 g/8 oz mixed berries,
such as blueberries,
raspberries and
strawberries, plus
extra to decorate

fresh mint sprigs,
to decorate (optional)

Method

1 Set the freezer to rapid freeze at least 2 hours
before freezing this dish. Line a 12-hole bun tin
with 12 paper cake cases, or use small ramekin
dishes placed on a baking sheet.

2 Mix the yogurt and orange zest together in
a large bowl. Cut any large strawberries into
pieces so that they are the same size as the
blueberries and raspberries.

3 Add the fruit to the yogurt then spoon into the
paper cases or ramekins. Freeze for 2 hours, or
until just frozen. Decorate with extra fruit and
mint sprigs, if using, and serve. Remember to
return the freezer to its original setting afterwards.

DESSERTS & BAKING

CHIA SEED &
BANANA ICE LOLLIES

Makes: 6

Prep: 20 mins,
plus freezing

Cook: No cooking

Ingredients

3 large ripe bananas

3 tbsp Greek-style
natural yogurt

2 tsp runny honey

2 tsp chia seeds

You will also need

6 x 50 ml/2 fl oz
ice lolly moulds

6 ice lolly sticks

Method

1 Blend the bananas, Greek yogurt and honey
in a blender or food processor until you have a
thick, smooth consistency. Stir in the chia seeds.

2 Transfer the mixture to a jug and pour the
mixture evenly into the six ice lolly moulds.

3 Place a lolly stick in the centre of each mould.
Place in the freezer and leave to freeze for 6
hours before serving.

4 To unmould the lollies, dip the frozen moulds
into warm water for a few seconds and gently
release the lollies while holding the sticks.

CRANBERRY & RASPBERRY JELLY

Serves: 6

Prep: 15 mins,
plus cooling & freezing

Cook: 15 mins

Ingredients

350 g/12 oz frozen cranberries

85 g/3 oz golden caster sugar

600 ml/1 pint water, plus extra for the gelatine

15 g/½ oz leaf gelatine

175 g/6 oz frozen raspberries, plus a few extra to serve

Method

1 Put the cranberries, sugar and 225 ml/8 fl oz of the water in a saucepan, cover and cook over a medium heat for 10–15 minutes. Leave to cool. Meanwhile, put the gelatine sheets in a shallow dish, cover with cold water and leave to soften for 5 minutes. Pour the cranberries and their cooking liquid into a food processor and process to a purée. Push the purée through a sieve back into the saucepan, then stir in the remaining water and warm over a low heat. Drain the gelatine sheets, add to the warm cranberry mixture and stir until the gelatine is dissolved. Leave to cool.

2 Arrange a ring of raspberries in the base of a 1.2-litre/2-pint jelly mould, then spoon a little of the cranberry mixture over the top. Freeze for 15-20 minutes, until set. Pour half the remaining cranberry mixture into the mould and sprinkle with half the remaining raspberries, then chill in the refrigerator for 1 hour, until just set. Pour the remaining cranberry mixture into the mould sprinkle over the remaining raspberries. Chill in the refrigerator for 4–6 hours, or until set firm.

3 Dip the mould into a bowl of hot water, count to ten, then lift it out. Invert the mould onto a plate, then, holding the mould and the plate tightly, jerk to release the jelly and serve.

DESSERTS & BAKING

WARM WALNUT & ORANGE CAKE

Serves: 10   **Prep: 25 mins**   **Cook: 2¼ hrs**

Ingredients

3 large whole oranges (approx 250 g/9 oz each)

125 g/4½ oz dried apricots

70 g/2½ oz walnuts, roughly chopped, plus 12 halves to decorate

70 g/2½ oz unblanched almonds, roughly chopped, plus 6 to decorate

70 g/2½ oz Brazil nuts, roughly chopped, plus 12 to decorate

4 eggs

200 g/7 oz golden caster sugar

125 ml/4 fl oz light olive oil, plus extra to grease

85 g/3 oz brown rice flour

2 tsp gluten-free baking powder

250 g/9 oz fat-free Greek-style natural yogurt, to serve

Method

1 Put one orange in a small saucepan, just cover with water, then bring to the boil, cover and simmer for 45 minutes. Add the dried apricots, re-cover and cook for 15 minutes, or until the orange is very tender. Drain the fruits, reserving the cooking water, and leave to cool. Preheat the oven to 160°C/325°F/Gas Mark 3. Brush a 24-cm/9½-inch round springform cake tin with a little oil. Put the 70 g/2½ oz each of walnuts, almonds and Brazil nuts in a food processor, then process until ground. Tip into a mixing bowl.

2 Roughly chop the cooked orange, discard any pips, then put it and the apricots in the food processor and process into a coarse purée. Add the eggs, 150 g/5½ oz sugar and all the oil, and process until smooth. Spoon the brown rice flour and baking powder into the ground nuts and mix well. Tip into the food processor and process until smooth. Pour the cake mixture into the prepared tin, spread it level, and decorate with the walnut halves, whole almonds and whole Brazil nuts. Bake for 1–1¼ hours, or until browned.

3 Cut the peel and pith away from the remaining oranges. Cut between the membranes to release the segments. Measure 125 ml/4 fl oz of the reserved orange cooking water, adding extra water if needed, and pour into a saucepan.

Add the remaining sugar and cook over a low heat until dissolved. Increase the heat to high and boil for 3 minutes, or until you have a syrup. Add the orange segments and leave to cool. Loosen the edge of the cake and turn out onto a wire rack. Leave to cool slightly, then cut into wedges. Serve warm, with the oranges in syrup and the Greek yogurt.

★ Variation

To make this extra special add four plump figs, cut into segments, to the top of the cake. Then sprinkle with 30 g/1 oz flaked, toasted almonds and the zest of one orange.

SUMMER BERRY SPONGE CAKES

Makes: 6

Prep: 25 mins, plus cooling

Cook: 15 mins

Ingredients

oil, to grease

3 eggs

85 g/3 oz golden caster sugar

½ tsp vanilla extract

85 g/3 oz brown rice flour

250 g/9 oz fat-free Greek-style natural yogurt

400 g/14 oz mixed raspberries, blueberries, and hulled and sliced strawberries

1 tbsp icing sugar, sifted

Method

1 Preheat the oven to 180°C/350°F/Gas Mark 4. Brush 6 x 175-ml/6-fl oz ring mould tins with a little oil and put them on a baking sheet.

2 Put the eggs, caster sugar and vanilla extract in a large bowl and beat with an electric hand-held whisk for 5 minutes, or until the mixture is thick and leaves a trail when the whisk is lifted.

3 Sift the flour over the egg mixture, then gently fold it in with a large metal spoon. Spoon the mixture into the tins and ease it into an even layer, being careful not to knock out any air.

4 Bake for 12–15 minutes, or until the cakes are risen and golden brown and beginning to shrink away from the edges.

5 Leave to cool in the tins for 5 minutes. Loosen the edges of the cakes with a round-bladed knife and turn them out onto a wire rack. Leave to cool completely.

6 Put the cakes on serving plates, spoon the yogurt into the centre, then pile the fruits on top. Dust with sifted icing sugar and serve.

RHUBARB & LEMON DRIZZLE SQUARES

Makes: 9

Prep: 30–35 mins, plus cooling

Cook: 35–40 mins

Ingredients

300 g/10½ oz trimmed young rhubarb, cut into 2-cm/¾-inch thick slices

100 g/3½ oz ground almonds

115 g/4 oz brown rice flour

1½ tsp baking powder

1 ripe banana, mashed

150 ml/5 fl oz rice bran oil

115 g/4 oz light muscovado sugar

grated zest of 1 lemon

3 eggs

25 g/1 oz unblanched almonds, roughly chopped

Syrup

juice of 2 lemons

60 g/2¼ oz light muscovado sugar

Method

1 Preheat the oven to 180°C/350°F/Gas Mark 4. Line a 30 x 20 x 4-cm/12 x 8 x 1½-inch square cake tin with a piece of non-stick baking paper.

2 Place the rhubarb in a dry roasting tin and bake in the preheated oven for 10 minutes, until almost soft. Remove from the oven but do not switch the oven off.

3 Put the ground almonds, flour and baking powder into a bowl and stir together.

4 Put the banana, oil, sugar and lemon zest into a separate bowl and whisk together until smooth. Whisk in the eggs, one at a time, then beat in the flour mixture.

5 Spoon the batter into the prepared tin, then scatter the rhubarb over the top. Bake for 25–30 minutes, until the cake is well risen and the sponge springs back when pressed with a fingertip.

6 To make the syrup, mix the lemon juice with the sugar. Spoon half over the hot cake and leave to soak in for 1–2 minutes. Spoon over the remaining syrup, scatter with the chopped almonds and leave to cool in the tin.

7 Lift the cake out of the tin, peel away the paper and cut into 9 small pieces.

HONEYED CARROT & PECAN SQUARES

Makes: 15   **Prep: 25 mins**   **Cook: 30 mins**

Ingredients

3 eggs

150 ml/5 fl oz virgin olive oil

115 g/4 oz light muscovado sugar

5 tbsp set honey

175 g/6 oz wholemeal plain flour

4 tbsp wheatgerm

2 tsp baking powder

2 tsp ground ginger

grated zest of 1 orange

1¼ tsp ground mixed spice

175 g/6 oz carrots, coarsely grated

55 g/2 oz pecan nuts, broken into pieces

Frosting

115 g/4 oz Greek-style natural yogurt

150 g/5½ oz cream cheese or mascarpone

Method

1 Preheat the oven to 180°C/350°F/Gas Mark 4. Line a 18 x 28 cm/7 x 11 inch roasting tin with with baking paper, snipping into the corners diagonally then pressing the paper into the tin so that both the base and sides are lined.

2 Crack the eggs into a large bowl, add the oil, sugar and 4 tablespoons of honey and whisk until smooth. Put the flour, wheatgerm and baking powder in a small bowl, then add the ginger, most of the orange zest and 1 teaspoon of mixed spice and stir. Add the dry ingredients to the egg mixture and whisk again until smooth. Add the carrots and most of the pecans and stir.

3 Spoon the mixture into the prepared tin and spread it into an even layer. Bake for 30 minutes, or until well risen and a skewer comes out cleanly when inserted into the centre. Remove the cake from the tin, peel off the baking paper and turn out onto a wire rack. Leave to cool.

4 To make the frosting, put the yogurt, cream cheese and remaining 1 tablespoon of honey and ¼ teaspoon of mixed spice into a bowl and beat until smooth. Spread the frosting over the cake, then sprinkle with the remaining pecans and orange zest. Cut into 15 squares and serve.

DESSERTS & BAKING

CARROT CAKE MUFFINS

Makes: 12

Prep: 15 mins,
plus cooling

Cook: 22 mins

Ingredients

10 g/¼ oz butter,
for greasing

90 g/3¼ oz wholemeal flour

60 g/2¼ oz plain flour

1 tsp bicarbonate of soda

1½ tsp ground cinnamon

½ tsp ground ginger

½ tsp salt

165 g/5¾ oz soft light
brown sugar

125 ml/4 fl oz unsweetened
apple sauce

4 tbsp sunflower oil

1 tsp vanilla extract

2 eggs, at room
temperature

2 carrots, finely shredded

35 g/1¼ oz raisins

25 g/1 oz walnuts, chopped

Method

1 Preheat the oven to 180°C/350°F/Gas Mark 4 and grease a 12-hole muffin tin.

2 Put the wholemeal flour, plain flour, bicarbonate of soda, cinnamon, ginger and salt into a medium-sized bowl and mix to combine.

3 Put the sugar, apple sauce and oil into a separate bowl and beat with a hand-held electric mixer until well combined. Add the vanilla extract and then add the eggs, one at a time, beating well after each addition.

4 Add the dry mixture to the wet mixture and beat for 1 minute until just combined. Gently stir in the carrots, raisins and walnuts. Scoop the batter into the prepared tin.

5 Bake in the preheated oven for 20–22 minutes, or until a cocktail stick inserted into the centre of a muffin comes out clean. Leave to cool in the tin for a few minutes, then transfer the muffins to a wire rack and leave to cool completely. Serve warm or at room temperature.